Hire Education

What Every College Grad Should Know About Landing That First Job

$ $ $

John W. "Buddy" Hobart

What Every College Grad Should Know About Landing That First Job

By John W. Hobart

All rights reserved. No part of this book may be reproduced or transmitted in any for or by any means, electronic or mechanical, including photocopying, recording or by a information storage and retrieval system without written permission from the publish Brief passages (not to exceed 1,000 words) may be quoted for reviews.

This publication is designed to provide accurate and authoritative information in rega to the subject matter covered. Its purpose is to educate and entertain. The author and Lighthouse Point Press shall have neither liability nor responsibility to any person or entity with respect to any loss or damage caused, or alleged to be caused, directly or indirectly by the information contained in this book.

Copyright © 1998 by John W. Hobart
Printed in the United States of America
Library of Congress Catalog Card Number 98-067138

Publisher's Cataloging in Publication Data
Hobart, John W., 1959 -
Hire Education: What Every College Grad Should Know About Landing That First Job / by John W. Hobart
     p.   cm.

Includes index.
1. Career
2. Reference
ISBN 0-9637966-5-8: $16.95 Softcover

Book Design by John McCue Advertising Design Consultants
This book is printed on acid-free stock.

First Printing, October 1998

Published by:

 Lighthouse Point Press
Riverside Commons
700 River Avenue
Pittsburgh, PA 15212

Copyright© 1998 John W. Hobart
ALL RIGHTS RESERVED

DEDICATION

This book is dedicated to David L. Maloney, without whose leadership, guidance and friendship, I never would have graduated.

P.S. Coach, Dad would have approved.

ACKNOWLEDGMENTS

Writing this book has been a labor of love. While I have enjoyed the writing process and the subject matter a great deal, what I enjoyed most was meeting the many students along the way. I am particularly grateful to Dr. Joseph Rudman and his business communications class at Carnegie Mellon University. Their fresh ideas and critical feedback were invaluable.

My friend, Bob Perrin, also deserves a very sincere thank you. Bob is a human resource expert and his contributions to this book were many. He will be happy to tell you that the parts you enjoy are his, everything else is mine.

Finally, a very special thank you goes out to Michelle Cerqua. Her constant encouragement and inspiration are the only reasons this book was ever completed.

Table of Contents

INTRODUCTION I

THE EVOLUTION OF BUSINESS 1
- Taking Inventory

PACKAGING YOUR PRODUCT 11
- Creating a Job Objective
- Controlling Your Airwaves

PRODUCT KNOWLEDGE 29
- Getting to Know Yourself
- Practice

MARKET KNOWLEDGE 71
- Creative Research
- Communication Skills

PROSPECTING 89
- Identifying Potential Employers
- Networking
- Implementing Your "One Step Away" List
- Seeking Advice Over the Telephone

THE INTERVIEW 113
- Non-Verbal Communication
- Professional Dress
- The Handshake
- Tone of Voice
- Interpersonal Communication
- Problem Solving
- Producing Results

CLOSING THE SALE 141
- The Dream Retirement Method (DRM)

SETTING YOURSELF APART 153

TAKING CONTROL 165
- Take Control...Today

Introduction

I graduated from college in 1981. At that time, I was under the impression that I should know exactly what I wanted to do next. College was supposed to prepare me for my future. After four years I should have heard my life's calling. Was I the only one who didn't answer the phone when life called? All my roommates, teammates and classmates seemed to know exactly what they wanted out of life. Why didn't I?

The cold, hard fact was that no one really knew what they wanted to do with their lives. There is no call — no phone call, wake-up call, port of call or any other call. Everyone thought they should know, so they acted like they did know. I am not aware of a single classmate who, 20 years later, is doing exactly what he or she set out to do upon graduation.

Let me share with you some highlights from my academic career. In my freshman year, I was required to take several "core" courses. I thought this was the greatest idea in the world. The college would pick my courses for the next four years. All I had to do was go along for the ride while the school guided me in the right direction.

I realized this was not the case when, in my sophomore year, it came time to declare a major. This was the first clue that I had no idea what I wanted to be when I graduated. Now comes true confession time: I did not even choose my own major. My academic advisor set up an appointment with me in his office. As soon as I sat down, he informed me that he had found a major that he thought I could manage.

To this day, I still wonder why he only thought I could manage it.

Shortly thereafter, I chose a second major and proceeded to learn a great deal about public policy, management and history during my final three years of college. Once I graduated, however, I went into a field that had nothing to do with my degree.

Even though I did not pursue a career in my major, college did prepare me for my future. College taught me how to think, study and learn. Most importantly, college taught me that I could overcome obstacles and uncertainty.

You might be feeling very uncertain yourself right now. That is why I want you to know that you are not alone. You may feel like you are the only one who does not have a definitive plan for the future. But you are not alone. I can attest to that.

In Salerno, Italy, during the ninth century, the first college graduated its first class. That class and every class since has asked the same deep, burning question:

"Now What?"

This book will not help you find your life's calling, but it definitely will help you find your first "real" job. The concepts, ideas, strategies and exercises in this book are all designed to address your needs as a college student entering the job market.

Hire Education will be different from any other book you may have read for two reasons: (1) It is designed to address job hunting in today's work world; and (2) It is written specifically for you, the college student. My career has afforded me many opportunities to learn about how college students should effectively market themselves. I want to share this information with you.

Since college, I have spent my career in sales and marketing. My first job was with Xerox Corporation as a major account salesperson. Early in my career, I was exposed to some of the finest marketing training in the world. After a few years with Xerox, I left to join a smaller regional firm, eventually being promoted to district manager. My position required a great deal of interviewing and hiring for all types of positions. During my time as a manager, I clearly saw the correlation between sales/marketing skills and the job search.

At about this same time, I began to teach at colleges about the job search process and ways in which college students can make a smooth transition into the working world. I've presented these courses to students at all levels of higher education, from those seeking associate's degrees to students completing master's work. *Hire Education* contains the information presented during these courses, as well as what I have learned from the students. The shared experiences included here will be helpful to you as you begin your job search.

An evolution has taken place. The work environment is dramatically different today than it was 20 years ago. This evolution has changed how all business decisions are made and what jobs are available. Most importantly, it has changed how you must find and land your first job.

It stands to reason that if businesses are evolving and changing rapidly, so too are the processes that define those businesses. Two processes that have changed dramatically over the past few years are buying and hiring. The buying and hiring decision-makers of today are not the same as their counterparts of years ago.

Recognizing this fact led me to start my own company, Solutions 21, an organizational and skill development firm. Our first product was a sales and marketing course, Knowledge-Based Sales™ (KBS). KBS is designed to teach sales professionals how to connect with, and address, the needs of today's decision-maker. This course has been presented to sales professionals throughout the United States and 12 countries around the world. The results have been the same, whether the participants were from Chicago, London, Geneva or Sydney.

All sales professionals attending KBS learn two key points. First, no matter how much sales experience they may have, it will not necessarily apply to today's decision-maker. Second, sales/marketing tactics that worked as recently as five years ago, may be the exact opposite of what will work in the twenty-first century.

Introduction

The twenty-first century business decision-maker is faced with The Decision-Maker's Paradox: Decision-makers never have enough knowledge and they never, ever, have enough time. If you learn how to use this market reality to your advantage, your job search will prove rewarding.

The success of KBS can be attributed to one fact: it was created to target today's decision-maker. The same skills taught to sales professionals around the world have been adapted for your situation and are in this book. Landing your first job is a matter of learning and practicing job search skills designed for the twenty-first century job market.

–J.W.H.

Author's Note: Throughout this book, you are going to be asked to complete a few exercises (✎) or to just stop and think (⧖). When you see these instructions, please take a moment to either complete the exercise, or put down the book and think. This is your book, designed to help in your job search. Use it! Write in it, make notes in it, and allow it to be a tool in your job search. At the end of each chapter you will find space for note taking.

> *"A whopping 46 percent of Fortune 500 companies in 1980 cannot be found on the current list."*
>
> — Tom Peters,
> management guru

Chapter 1

The Evolution of Business

As a college student looking for your first job, you must understand today's job market for college graduates. The decade of the 1980s provided, for the most part, an excellent job market. By 1990, the market had shifted. Terms such as "rightsizing," "downsizing" and "re-engineering" had entered the business vernacular.

Firms scrambled to cut their work forces and save on expenses. Entry-level positions were eliminated at record rates. The number of companies looking to hire recent college graduates fell, and new entry-level positions were not created.

The mid-1990s saw the job market rebound, along with opportunities for recent college graduates. Between 1993 and 1994, the number of jobs for recent graduates rose for the first time since 1987.[1] Between 1994 and 2005, the overall job market is projected to increase 14 percent.[2] Jobs requiring at least an associate's degree will grow at a rate faster than the 14 percent average rate projected for all occupations.

While this is all good news for the graduating college student, competition for these jobs is also increasing.[3] In recent years, college enrollment has remained steady at historically high levels, which means fierce competition for jobs upon graduation. As we enter the twenty-first century, more than one million students earn bachelor's degrees each year, while another half million complete associate's degrees.[4] Those college graduates who can set themselves apart from the competition during the job search process will be the ones who will land the more desirable positions.

The first step in setting yourself apart from the competition is to understand who makes the hiring decisions. Today's decision-maker is dramatically different from his or her predecessor of years past. Changes in the economy and the work environment over the past two decades have affected every aspect of business. Organizations' hiring processes and decision-makers have also been impacted. Why are these professionals so different today? Why has the process changed so dramatically? How did the decision-maker of yesterday evolve into the decision-maker of the twenty-first century?

---

[1] L. Patrick Sheetz, Ph.D., Recruiting Trends 1996-97, 26th ed., (Michigan State University: Michigan, 1996).
[2] "BLS Releases New 1994 - 2005 Employment Projections," Bureau of Labor Statistics, on-line, 1 Dec. 1995.
[3] Harvey Mackay, Dig Your Well Before You're Thirsty (New York: Doubleday, 1997).
[4] Statistical Abstract of the United States, 1997, U.S. Department of Commerce, Economics and Statistics Administration, Bureau of the Census, (Washington, D.C., 1997).

In order to answer these questions, a quick history lesson will be helpful. The business environment of the twenty-first century did not happen instantaneously; it evolved. The end of World War II in 1945 gave way to a "Baby Boom," the largest population increase in U.S. history, which began the following year and lasted the better part of two decades. From 1946 to 1964, 50.1 million people were born.[5] The evolution of the business environment of the twenty-first century begins with these "Baby Boomers." They are the people now making the hiring decisions.

Unlike their parents, many Baby Boomers entered college. The first wave of Boomers began graduating from college by 1967 and entered the job market. Baby Boomers became not only the largest group of prospective employees in history, but also the best educated.

By the mid-1980s, the last wave of "Boomers" left college. From the mid-60s to the mid-80s, these graduates marketed themselves to a work world and a hiring decision-maker who existed at that time. The twenty-first century has produced a hiring process and decision-maker who is radically different from someone in the same position as recently as 10 or 15 years ago.

Why does any of this matter? This is why: As the Baby Boomers became successful in their job searches, and ultimately their careers, they began to teach the next generation of graduates how to find jobs. While this process was repeated from graduating class to graduating class, the profile of the hiring decision-maker was changing but the "job search training" was staying the same. As a graduate entering the twenty-first century work world, your job search/marketing campaign needs to be updated to keep pace with today's decision-maker's profile.

You must know the profile of your target audience to be successful in any marketing campaign. Who was the target audience, the decision-maker, for the Baby Boomer graduates? What was his profile?

---

[5]Campbell R. McConnell and Stanley L. Brue, Economics: Principles, Problems and Policies, 13th ed., (McGraw-Hill, Inc. 1996).

In our training courses held around the world, participants are asked to profile a "typical" decision-maker of the 1960 to 1980 era. Whether the decision-maker is from Nashville, New York, London, Toronto or Melbourne, the profile is the same:

Yesterday's Decision-Maker: 1960 – 1980

Born 1920s
White/male
Served in World War II
Financially conservative
Paid cash, not credit
Bought and kept items for long time

May be college educated
Traditional family makeup
Sole bread winner
Worked 9 to 5
One job for life
Promoted through the ranks

After the war, an economic expansion began, driven by the reality that after years of destruction the world needed to be rebuilt. Thousands of veterans returned home, found jobs and started families. Characteristically, a person in this group progressed until he ultimately became the decision-maker, deciding what to buy and sell ... and who to hire.

As a product of the Great Depression, "Yesterday's Decision-Maker" tended to be conservative and appreciated the value of money. The inappropriate use of credit and the failing of banks during the dark days of the 1930s taught him to handle his financial affairs with restraint. His military experience also shaped his management style. In the military, decisions are made very autocratically and Yesterday's Decision-Maker applied this approach to the business world.

As a business person of the 1950s and 1960s, Yesterday's Decision-Maker had very different tools at his disposal. Television was in its infancy, and the invention of the desktop personal computer was still decades in the future. There were no fax machines, overnight packages, e-mail or teleconferencing to speed up the pace of work. In a word, Yesterday's Decision-Maker was *tactical*. His decisions were based upon what could be seen and touched.

Baby Boomers entering the job market learned who this target market was and adjusted their job search accordingly. The hiring decisions were made by tactical thinkers; therefore, Baby Boomers incorporated job search tactics.

These tactics worked and Baby Boomers entered the work force in record numbers. Since they proved effective, they have been shared with every graduating class since 1965!

In some sense, job search tactics are tradition, passed from generation to generation. Tradition is a hard thing to change; however, in order to succeed in today's job search, you need to reexamine the target audience. Failure to do so will have you targeting a decision-maker who is over 75 years old today.

In contrast to the profile of Yesterday's Decision-Maker, here is a profile of "Today's Decision-Maker." Regardless of what developed country you are in, Today's Decision-Maker looks pretty much the same:

Today's Decision-Maker: Twenty-First Century

40ish	Possibly post graduate degree	Many jobs during career
Baby Boomer	Very time sensitive	Multi-cultural world view
Works 50+ hours per week	Male or female	Stressed by pace of work
Financially leveraged	Computer literate	
Well-traveled	Lives in disposable society	

Business people of the twenty-first century have a multitude of tools at their disposal. Personal computers, fax machines, teleconferencing, e-mail and a host of other high-tech gadgetry have combined to dramatically speed up the pace of work. Just as the tools have changed, so too has the profile of the decision-maker.

Today's Decision-Maker is far more diverse, educated and technologically-advanced than his or her predecessors. Furthermore, Today's Decision-Maker faces growing job demands and is thus perpetually strapped for time. It should come as no surprise that he or she is likely to change careers one or more times.

To survive in this environment, a professional must leverage ideas. A lever provides "added strength," allowing a person to lift a greater weight than would otherwise be possible. In business, leveraging ideas works the same way. A decision-maker can gain added strength by implementing the right concept at the right time.

In a word, Today's Decision-Maker must be *conceptual*. So, to be successful in your job search, you must incorporate new concepts that will appeal to Today's

Decision-Maker. Regardless of your career choice, the way hiring decisions are made has changed forever. The global marketplace, information technology and conceptual thinking have penetrated all work environments.

This point was really driven home for me during a business trip to Australia. On one of my off days I went to explore the outback. After several hours, I came across a general store in the middle of nowhere. There was a sign, "Last petrol for 300km." I decided to stop and fill the tank.

The storefront looked like something from a movie set. The dog sleeping on the old wood porch, cattle roaming behind the store, and the outhouse with no running water all served to give the place a "lost in time" feel. It seemed as if I were miles, and years, away from the twenty-first century.

After the owner filled my tank, I walked into the store to pay. Before the owner could pull out the cigar box that served as a cash register, he had to first close and move his laptop computer. Witnessing my amazement, he explained how "everything is changing and I need to keep up with the times."

What he said next is worth repeating! "The world is getting smaller and smaller. I must look at what I do well and fix what I don't, or I'm sure to fail." Even in Australia's outback, business people are realizing the need to adapt and apply concepts.

This book is designed to help you connect with Today's Decision-Maker. You will create your own job search marketing campaign. Your campaign will require you to learn a conceptual approach targeted to Today's Decision-Maker. In some cases, you will need to "re-learn" or disregard old tactics you may have been taught that were designed for Yesterday's Decision-Maker. The twenty-first century is upon us, and you need to adapt your job search skills to the evolution of business.

Taking Inventory

In addition to profiling the target audience, any successful marketing campaign addresses a product's strengths and weaknesses. As you begin your job search, it is critical that you identify your strengths and weaknesses.

Here's another way of looking at this situation: Imagine that you have decided not to work for someone else. Instead, you have decided to start your own business.

You have invented a one-of-a-kind product. All of your time has been spent improving it, polishing it, expanding its capabilities, and perfecting it for market.

Your product is such a valuable, high-ticket item that you will need only one sale to have a successful business. This one sale will be worth several million dollars, which will be paid to you in annual installments for the next 40 years. The product you have polished and perfected is, of course, YOU. Your job search is exactly like starting your own business, and only one sale is needed for success.

As you prepare to take your product to market, it is important to identify all your strengths and weaknesses. As with any product, you need to market your strengths and work to improve on your weaknesses.

First, you will need to take inventory of yourself and create lists of your strengths and weaknesses. On page 8 is a chart for this exercise. Before you begin, I suggest that you list the following as strength number one: COURAGE. Right now you may not be feeling courageous; however, this is a major attribute that cannot be ignored.

All your life you have been taught that courage is running into a burning building to save a baby. Certainly that is courageous, but there are also other forms of courage. People who run into burning buildings face their fears. They confront them, and then they take action. That is exactly what you're doing right now.

You had the courage to enroll in school. You had the courage to persevere. Reading this book is a sign of courage. You have the courage to admit you need help and to seek out that help.

Finally, like the hero rushing into the burning building, you have the courage to face your fears and take action. By reading this book, by preparing yourself, by accepting and overcoming your fears, you are displaying courage. Therefore, place COURAGE at the top of your list. Remember, nothing courageous ever happens until you make yourself vulnerable.

I want to prove to you that you have been afraid, faced that fear, and overcame your anxieties. Please take a few quiet moments and think about the following point. While you are doing this, do not just think about the events that occurred, but also think about the emotions, how you felt, and how you perceived the events around you.

⌛ Think about your first day at college. Were you frightened during your first day of school? Did you wonder how you were going to make it? Were you worried that you wouldn't meet new friends? Were some classes just going to be impossible? Were you afraid that you could not find your lab? Did you think that the English professor was never going to see your point of view?

How do you feel about these fears now? Were they realized? Have you still not found your lab? Were some of these fears simply based on the unknown? Looking back, don't you feel a bit silly that some of these were fears at all?

Five years from now, after you are secure in your career, you will feel the same way about your job search. Your lack of experience and a fear of the unknown is likely causing you to be anxious right now. The information and accompanying exercises are designed to help you bridge that experience gap. Just like the first day of school, your fears will subside with experience.

As you proceed with your job search, you'll need to call on all of your previous successes. You'll also have to rely on your number one strength — COURAGE.

This book is designed to help you prepare your product for market. It's a form of self-help book. Everyone who buys a self-help book desires self-improvement. They read the book, they absorb its message, and they want more than anything for it to work. That is why there are so many of these books.

Not everyone takes up the challenge to improve themselves. To do so yourself, you must access your courage. Throughout this book, and throughout your job search, you must do exactly that. You are a unique product, the only one like you that exists in the world. You have been perfected for market. You need make only one sale for your business to flourish for the next 40 years.

For the exercise below, take inventory of your marketable strengths and the areas you will need to improve upon in order to prepare yourself for the job market. You will be asked to refer back to this completed exercise later on in the book.

STRENGTHS	WEAKNESSES
1. COURAGE	1.
2.	2.
3.	3.
4.	4.
5.	5.
6.	6.
7.	7.
8.	8.
9.	9.
10.	10.
11.	11.
12.	12.
13.	13.
14.	14.
15.	15.
16.	16.
17.	17.
18.	18.
19.	19.
20.	20.

Notes for *Taking Inventory:*

> "Develop advertising as good as the product."
>
> — Leo Burnett,
> advertising executive

Chapter 2

Packaging Your Product

Creating a Job Objective

The evolution of business has brought about an evolution of business practices. The corporate world has begun to embrace many different concepts in order to compete in the global economy. In the early 1990s, the trend was toward "rightsizing" — the reduction of a firm's work force by attrition, layoffs or employee buyouts. Rightsizing, as well as other business concepts, will likely have a direct impact on your job search.

Britain's Institute of Management conducted a survey designed to identify the top management tools used throughout the world. Four distinct global regions were surveyed: North America, the United Kingdom, Europe and Asia. While there were slight differences in the survey results, a common set of management goals rose to the surface: to address customer satisfaction, to improve quality, to work as a team, and to do all of these quickly. Like rightsizing, these objectives also will affect your job search.

Your competition is different now than it was for a graduate 10 years ago. Also, those in the work world are now forced to "do more with less." This means that people who make hiring decisions do not have enough time, or at least, they do not have any time to waste. These two factors, competition and time, are critical. Your competition for a job might be someone with several years work experience. You will not always be competing with other recent graduates. Therefore, you will need to leverage the second factor — time. In Chapter 9, we will discuss additional ways these management trends can be used to your advantage.

In the current work environment, business decision-makers are constantly pressed for time. Everything you do, at every step of the process, must show respect for their time. This starts with your résumé. Every product needs a brochure. Since you are now concentrating on selling yourself as the product, you should think of your résumé as your brochure.

In your library, college bookstore, and especially your school's placement office, there are many books designed to help you write a résumé and a cover letter. On page 170 are my recommendations. Read one of these books, and as soon as possible make an appointment to see a career counselor in the placement office. Ask him or her to help you write a résumé. You will find that the placement office will prove invaluable during your job search.

Right now, you are only going to concern yourself with the opening line of your résumé: the job objective. The importance of a job objective cannot be understated, as this one line can make or break your chances early in the hiring process. To help you understand the importance of a job objective, I would like to bring you around to my side of the desk. As a person who has done a great deal of hiring, I have spent a lot of time reviewing résumés. I want to share with you the "real world" view of résumés.

Let's set the stage. It is a Wednesday evening at 6 p.m. I need to evaluate a four-and-one-half-inch stack of résumés sitting on the corner of my desk. These résumés need to be reviewed before my staff meeting at 8 a.m. tomorrow. I am looking to hire two salespeople and I want to narrow the search to 15 candidates.

In today's competitive work environment, this task is a "B" priority — one that could be accomplished after hours. I am forced to do more with less, so my work day has expanded nearly 20 percent. I have already put in 10 1/2 hours by 6 p.m.

You may not see a problem with this situation. After all, it is only 6 p.m., and as a dedicated, hard-working individual, I certainly would be willing to work all night to review these résumés. However, there are two major points I have not shared with you.

First of all, last week I was out of town for three days, and I will be traveling again next week. I have not had two days off in a row for over a month, using my weekends as travel days to the west coast and Europe. My recent schedule has included four trips into different time zones and a trip across the international dateline. Needless to say, I am tired. To make matters worse, there is no end in sight.

Second, I am determined to find a few moments for myself. Tonight presents a perfect opportunity. The country's number one- and number two-ranked college basketball teams are scheduled to play on television at 8 p.m. If at all possible, I would like to relax with this relatively mindless activity and re-energize myself. I need some time away from work. Since it is already 6 p.m., I have only two hours between now and tip-off. It takes me 15 minutes to get from the office to my home. If I want to get home, change clothes, and relax in front of the television, I will need to leave my office by 7:30.

I also would like some chips and dip for the game. I am going to need an extra 10 minutes to stop at the store. Keep in mind my recent work schedule and my determination to get in a few hours of relaxation. Suddenly, what appeared to be an all-night task has been narrowed down to one hour and 20 minutes. I cannot spend more than a few seconds with each résumé.

How am I going to conquer this mountain of résumés in 80 minutes? I am going to look at each résumé's job objective. The job objective will tell me immediately if the person is interested in the available position.

Now let's begin to go through the stack of résumés. The first résumé has no job objective. I'll put that over here in the rejection letter pile. The next several résumés have no job objective. I place all of them in the rejection pile. Finally, a job objective, "I am seeking a position with a growing firm in a competitive marketplace where I can utilize my work experience, educational background and knowledge of three different languages."

Sound familiar? While impressive, the objective does not tell me anything. In an attempt to cover all of your bases, you might be tempted to put together a job objective that covers everything. You certainly do not want to limit yourself. But remember how the scenario has been set. The person reviewing these résumés has only an hour and 20 minutes to spend with them.

By not being specific with your job objective, you are requiring the person reviewing the résumé to read the entire document. In other words, having too general a job objective accomplishes the same thing as having no job objective. Your goal is to show that you want what the prospective employer is offering.

Next résumé. No objective. Rejection letter. Next résumé. No objective. Rejection letter. Next résumé. A job objective that states, "I am seeking a position in sales and marketing." At this point, I will spend no more than ten seconds reviewing this résumé to see if the person's qualifications measure up to the desired objective. If they do, I will place it in my pile of 15 future candidates.

The most important and eye-catching part of your résumé is the job objective. You will set yourself apart, and increase your odds by including a succinct job objective. Your competition may well have more experience, maybe even a better educational background, but without a job objective, they have taken themselves out of the running. Given my time constraints, your job objective will get my attention. Your competition's lack of one will get him or her a rejection letter.

The Electronic Age has done nothing to negate the need for a job objective. If you are e-mailing your résumé, do not think that an objective is unnecessary. While the transmission may be done electronically, the decision about your résumé will still be made by a person. The same time constraint rules apply.

The employee resource director for a Fortune 500 company recently added a page to the company's Web site for recruiting. He said that it is not a prominent part of the Web site, nor is it the site's primary purpose. Nevertheless, on the first day he received 12 résumés. Since then he has received hundreds of inquiries and expects thousands of résumés in the near future.

Once the director receives a résumé, the first thing he looks at is the job objective. If there is a succinct objective, he immediately forwards the résumé to the proper hiring manager. Résumés with no job objective are catalogued by geography based on the person's address. These résumés are held for six months and then discarded. Rarely will they be used again in the hiring process.

Why are you uncomfortable writing a specific job objective? Did you answer, "I don't want to limit myself" or "I'm not sure what I want to do?"

You need to package your product in order to sell it in several different markets. Narrow your focus to a handful of job objectives and have each printed on a separate résumé. **Print a different résumé for each job objective.**

Are you thinking, "What?! Print several different résumés with several different job objectives! Isn't this unethical? Shouldn't I know what I want to do when I graduate? How can I send the same résumé to different people with different job objectives? This whole idea sounds strange and unfair."

Remember, this is your brochure. It is intended to target a specific market. A brochure, or commercial, is only designed to get the consumer to look at, demonstrate, or more strongly consider — buying the product. Simply put, a brochure's purpose is to create interest. Let's take a look at how other products are positioned in their target markets.

Pay attention to the commercials the next time you are watching television. Turn on a football game. Sometime during the football game you're going to see a commercial for a luxury car. During this commercial, the focus will be on how well the car handles and how quickly it goes from 0 to 50 mph. Visually, you may see it on the highway traveling at a high rate of speed, or taking sharp curves on a dime. Keep this commercial in mind the next time you are watching a prime time program.

Sometime during the prime time show you may see a commercial for the same luxury car; however, in this commercial you will see it pull up in front of a beautiful home. Out of the car will step a very distinguished-looking gentleman, who will walk around to the other side and open the door for a very elegant woman. He will close the door behind her and they will proceed into the beautiful house. Throughout the entire commercial, the announcer will only talk about the luxury and prestige of the automobile.

Why would a car manufacturer have two distinctly different commercials for the same car? Why aren't these commercials "flip-flopped," with the luxury commercial broadcast during the football game, and the handling-abilities commercial shown on the movie of the week?

Never has it been unethical for a car manufacturer to position its product differently, based on the market. Nor is it unethical for you to position your product in the same manner. Therefore, write several job objectives that can be positioned within the markets you are targeting.

Many very qualified people receive rejection letters. In fact, it is a myth that the most qualified person gets the job. The people who best represent their qualifications get the jobs. Having a job objective will increase the odds of having an overworked and time-conscious decision-maker review your qualifications. If your objective and qualifications match their needs, you are one step closer to being hired.

If you are unsure of which job objective/résumé to send, call the company and ask for someone in human resources (HR). If there is no HR department, ask for the person who does the initial interviewing. If all else fails, ask the receptionist. Explain your situation and ask for help. You will be amazed at how helpful most people will be.

Sometimes you cannot call the company directly to find out which résumé to send. In that case, you will simply have to make an educated guess. You might guess correctly. If not, your odds of success are still greater than if you send a résumé without an objective.

If you receive a rejection letter after you have submitted your résumé, try again in a few weeks. Change occurs quickly in most organizations, and your timing might be perfect.

In order to develop your résumé, you must expand your strengths and weaknesses into a complete self-inventory. This inventory will be useful as you prepare for, and ultimately participate in interviews.

✎ Below is a self-inventory exercise. Take some time to think before filling in each category. Refer to your strengths and weaknesses on page 8 as well as "What Employers Look For" and "Why Employers Will Pay More" on page 18.

Self-Inventory

Interests
What are your interests? What do you enjoy?

? _____
? _____
? _____
? _____
? _____

Skills
What are your skills? In what areas do you excel?

? _____
? _____
? _____
? _____
? _____

Work Experiences
What are your work experiences and how have these benefited you?

? _____
? _____
? _____
? _____
? _____

Most Enjoyed Classes/Experiences

What classes/experiences did you most enjoy? How can you apply these to your job search?

? _____
? _____
? _____
? _____
? _____

Leadership Experiences

In what instances have you used leadership skills?

? _____
? _____
? _____
? _____
? _____

Team Building Experiences

How have you interacted with others academically, athletically or in your work experiences?

? _____
? _____
? _____
? _____
? _____

Career Choices

What do you want to do with your career?

? _____
? _____
? _____
? _____
? _____

What Employers Look For

Academic course work

College degree

Campus experiences

Internships

Co-operative education assignment

Part-time work experiences

Leadership roles

Volunteer work experiences

Team activities

Campus/community involvement

Tasks requiring people skills

Analytical thinking activities

Clubs and student activities that promote:

- Academics
- Enterprise
- Passion for hard work
- Ability to plan
- Capacity to organize
- Competence for analytical thinking

Why Employers Will Pay More

Prior work experience

Co-operative education assignment

Internships

Career-related summer employment

Academic achievement

Participation in school activities

Leadership roles in student organizations

Perceived potential within hiring organization

Source: Twenty-Sixth Edition Recruiting Trends, "A Study of Businesses, Industries, and Governmental Agencies Employing New College Graduates."

Once you have completed the self-inventory exercise, it is time to develop your job objective.

Sample Job Objectives

I am seeking a management-trainee position in sales and marketing.
I am seeking an entry-level accounting position.
I am seeking a full-time administrative position.

Résumé Outline

Recent Graduate

Name: _____

School Address: Permanent Address:
_____   _____
_____   _____
_____   _____

Career Objective:
_____

Education:
_____
_____

Pertinent Courses:
_____   _____
_____   _____
_____   _____

Work Experience:
Position:
_____

Responsibilities/duties at the above position:
_____
_____
_____

Publications, Awards, Achievements:
_____
_____
_____

References available upon request.

Résumé Outline

Previous Work Experience

Name: _____

School Address: Permanent Address:
_____   _____
_____   _____
_____   _____

Career Objective:
_____

Work Experience:
Position:
_____

Responsibilities/duties at the above position:
_____
_____
_____

Education:
_____
_____

Pertinent Courses:
_____   _____
_____   _____
_____   _____

Publications, Awards, Achievements:
_____
_____
_____

References available upon request.

Résumé Outline

Recent Graduate

Name: _____
Address: _____
City, State Zip: _____
Telephone Number: _____
E-mail Address: _____

Objective:
_____

Education:
_____
_____

Courses Taken:
_____   _____
_____   _____

Employment:
Position: _____
Location: _____
Dates: _____
Responsibilities/duties at the above position(s):
_____
_____
_____
_____

Community Activities/Achievements:
_____
_____
_____
_____

References available upon request.

Résumé Outline

Previous Work Experience

Name: _____
Address: _____
City, State Zip: _____
Telephone Number: _____
E-mail Address: _____

Objective:
_____

Employment:

Position: _____
Location: _____
Dates: _____
Responsibilities/duties at the above position(s):
_____
_____
_____
_____

Education:
_____
_____

Courses Studied:

_____   _____
_____   _____
_____   _____

Community Activities/Achievements:
_____
_____
_____
_____

References available upon request.

Controlling Your Airwaves

You have completed your brochures and are ready to take your product to market. From here on out, everything you do will reflect on your marketability. You cannot afford to project the wrong image.

Controlling your "airwaves" means controlling your answering machine. (If you do not have an answering machine, invest in one.) Consider the following sample messages. What image does each convey?

Think of the following message in the "I'm the coolest guy in the world" voice. Message One: "You called, leave a message and I might call you back."

Think of the following message in the highest-pitched voice possible. Message Two: "Hi. Tammy, Bobby Joe and I are probably skipping class. Since we're not here, we're probably out working on our tans, so leave a message and we'll get back to ya!"

Think of the following message in a very professional tone. Message Three: "Hello, you've reached 555-2121. I'm unable to come to the phone right now, but if you leave your name and number, I'll get back to you as quickly as possible."

Now, again let's bring you around to the other side of the desk. To a prospective employer, which of the above messages would best represent you? In other words, which of these three would an employer find most appropriate? At 7:15 p.m., when I am ready to go home, will I really be in the right frame of mind to appreciate an unprofessional message?

⧖ Your goal is to increase your odds at every step along the way. If you submit a great résumé, with perfect credentials, and an employer calls and hears an unprofessional message, have you helped or hurt your chances?

The best illustration of the need for a succinct job objective and proper control of your airwaves is also a very poignant example of the global marketplace. A friend, Raymond Wiley, shares this story:

"As a part of my job, I was constantly sourcing recent college graduates and candidates for summer intern positions. My job required me to travel a great deal and I would often review résumés on the run. Given my time constraints, jet lag and the demands of my position, the first thing I looked for was a job objective. If there was no objective, I would not even read the résumé.

"Once I narrowed down the résumés to the best prospects, I would often follow up myself by telephone. When calling the United States, I had to contend with a time difference. In order to reach a prospective candidate during the day, I would have to call late at night.

"After a trip from Malaysia to Tokyo, I did not want to stay up all night on the telephone. If I could not reach someone because they did not have an answering machine, I would seldom find the time to call back. Likewise, if a person's message was unprofessional, I was instantly turned off. I understand college is fun, but at 1 a.m., and working on tight deadlines, I had to maximize my time and resources accordingly."

Look at the three sample answering machine messages again. Examine the first two. A prospective employer might overlook these messages. The key word is "might." There are no guarantees. Look at the third message. Is it offensive in any way? This message would not turn off a prospective employer. Finally, examine the messages from the caller's perspective. At every step of the job-search process, you must be aware of, and show respect for the prospective employer's time. The third message shows this respect.

In the area below, write your own recorded message. Be concise, professional and show respect for the caller's time. Practice your message several times before recording. Be natural and avoid any verbal noise ("ums", hesitations, music in the background, etc.). If you sound too mechanical or are not happy with the recording for any reason, record it again.

Your Answering Machine Script:

"Hello,

_____

_____

_____

_____

"Hello,

_____

_____

_____

_____

Notes for *Packaging Your Product:*

Notes for *Packaging Your Product:*

> *"The first rule of winning:
> don't beat yourself."*
> — Football adage

Chapter 3

Product Knowledge

Getting to Know Yourself

One of the age-old fallacies associated with the interviewing process is that the interviewer holds all the cards. Preparing for an interview might seem impossible, as someone else will be directing the session. But this is not true. The most important preparation that can be done for an interview is to study yourself. The reality of an interview is that you are in control. To a certain extent, the interviewer will take the lead; however, if you are prepared, you can assume control and determine the ultimate outcome.

⌛ Think about a test you took that resulted in a good grade. Did you study and prepare for this exam? Were you confident of the material and your ability to present it under pressure? While you may have been a bit nervous taking the test, did your nervousness affect your ability to achieve a good grade?

⌛ Now think about a test that did not go so well. Were you as confident that you had the material "down cold?" Were you as prepared as possible? Was your nervousness associated with this exam different? Did your nervousness get in the way of your ability to perform well on the test? What difference did thorough preparation make?

Preparing yourself for an interview is the same as preparing yourself for final exams. In many respects, the interview is like taking an open-book test. One major difference is that you are the only one who knows the correct answers. If you prepare properly for this test, you will dramatically increase your chances for success.

In a perfect world, everyone who interviews has spent 15 or 20 years studying how to properly conduct an interview. The cold, hard reality is that most interviewers have never received any training. Since most interviewers are "winging it," they are not very good.

In the age of rightsizing, downsizing and horizontal organization charts, an interviewer may have been called upon to "fill in" and conduct some interviews, or he or she may have been promoted recently into a role that requires interviewing. Therefore, this person may be completely unprepared to conduct a solid and thorough interview. By preparing your product knowledge you will be able to master an interview session, whether with a good or not-so-good interviewer.

Ideally, an interview will consist of several broad areas. And a good interviewer will lead you, in detail, through each of these areas. A not-so-good interviewer will bounce around from area to area and not create any continuity throughout the session.

You are going to need to understand each of these areas in order to take control and manage the interview process. These areas are your personal life chapters, or "funnels."

Look at each area, or chapter of your life as a funnel. Information will start on top in a broad general way, and continue until it has been narrowed down to more specific information. These funnels are as follows:

Personal background information. Who are you? Where are you from? Where did you go to high school? Why did you choose your college?

Evaluation of educational background. What have you studied? What types of courses have you taken? What experiences have you had in school? What is your major? Do you have any minors and how do they relate?

Activities and organizations. Are you a member of any clubs, fraternities, sororities or charitable organizations? Do you hold any responsible positions in these organizations?

Work experience. What jobs have you held and why? Have these experiences provided you with opportunities to show responsibility? Did you hold summer jobs in order to pay for your education? Have your summer jobs provided you with any relevant experience?

Career goals. What are you looking to do when you graduate? What direction would you like your career/professional life to take? What are your goals?

Several exercises at the end of this chapter will help you prepare for your funnels. So to better understand how these funnels work, let's examine the process more closely.

Let's pretend that you are out on a Friday night. As luck would have it, you spot an individual you would just love to "get to know better." This person approaches you and begins to break the ice with some small talk, "Where are you from? Do you go to school around here? What's your major?"

⌛ How would you respond to these questions? Would you follow them up with questions of your own? Would your questions be based on his or her last response or would you "bounce around?"

If you are attempting to "get to know someone," your conversation would flow smoothly. Your responses would be based on their questions and your follow-up questions would flow from all previous conversation. You would not bounce around from subject to subject.

To avoid bouncing around during an interview, you must understand each funnel. In the first funnel, the interviewer may want to discuss your personal background (personal history, where you're from, hobbies, etc.) at the beginning of the interview. This may be done just to break the ice and to get a feel for how you respond to questions.

The second funnel, which may take much more time, is your educational background. How did you choose your college or university? How did you choose your major? What is your career choice? What are you studying? What courses did you enjoy? What courses didn't you enjoy? Why?

The third funnel is activities and organizations. As you prepare yourself to work through this funnel, concentrate on questions such as: What kinds of organizations did you belong to on campus or outside of school? What responsibilities did you assume within these organizations? Did you hold any elected offices? What were your responsibilities? Were you a leader? Did you function well within the team environment? The interviewer will want to know how these areas complement your other funnels.

The fourth funnel is work experience. You should be prepared to discuss the types of jobs you have had in the past. How much time did you spend in each of the positions? What types of responsibilities did you assume? What did you learn? Did you supervise/train other people? How did you handle independent responsibilities?

Within this funnel, do not be afraid to discuss jobs you've held that were not relevant to your career choice but allowed you to earn money that you applied toward your education. Interviewers understand and respect the need to finance one's education. If this was the case, be prepared to discuss how this has proven to be a major benefit to your overall growth and development.

The fifth funnel will be your career goals. You should be candid and clear about what you are looking to do with your career. If you are familiar with career tracks within the interviewing organization, be prepared to draw parallels to your own goals. You may want to question the interviewer on his or her own career path. This might give you insight into the company's expectations.

If you already have experience with interviewers, then you already know some are better than others. Some interviewers immediately make you feel comfortable and seem to have a conversational flow to their questioning. Other interviewers might jump around and never quite make you feel comfortable.

When faced with a poor interviewer, people tend to interview poorly. It's just that simple. But a poor interviewer is not an excuse for interviewing poorly. Do not console yourself into believing that it was the interviewer's fault.

If you interview poorly, even with a poor interviewer, it is YOU who does not get the job. It is your responsibility to assume the necessary control in order to have a good interview.

A few years ago, a former business associate of mine applied for a position with one of the nation's largest accounting firms. She was successful in her initial round of interviews and eventually was asked to meet with one of the firm's senior partners.

Very early into the interview, my friend realized that this person, while very bright and successful, was not skilled in the interviewing process. He really was struggling to find the proper format. After a brief period, the senior partner asked my friend to share her work experience.

Seizing the opportunity and having knowledge of the funnel process, my friend suggested that she could share her entire background in the following areas: education, activities and organizations, work experience and future career goals. The entire conversation lasted about 25 minutes.

My friend did get the position, and early into her new job she was informed that she was offered the position in part because the senior partner, who had made the final decision, was extremely impressed with her thought processes and organizational skills when he interviewed her.

In the beginning of this book, I stated one thing that I already knew about you: you are courageous. There is another thing I know: not only are you courageous, but you also assume control and accountability. If you didn't, you would not be reading this book and working to improve yourself. You have assumed the accountability necessary to be successful. With this in mind, I want you to realize you can take control of an interviewing situation, even with a bad interviewer.

You should quickly evaluate the interviewer, and his or her personality and interviewing style. This is no different than any other interaction you have ever had in your life. Your ability to determine how you're going to interact with an individual needs to be applied to the interviewing process.

If you are confronted with an interviewing situation that appears to be headed nowhere, **take control**. Once you know your funnels, it will be easy to assume control. The process will go something like this:

"Why don't I take you through my résumé and start by outlining a few things from my personal background, talk a little about my education, my outside activities and some of the previous jobs I've held. After that, I'd like to talk to you about why I am interested in XYZ Corporation and what I hope to accomplish here. And finally, if you don't mind, I may have a few questions for you about XYZ Corporation."

The funnel process, whether implemented consciously or unconsciously, is a fairly standard process used by interviewees at all levels. Being familiar with the process in advance allows you to be much more comfortable and make the best use of the available time. Most interviews, especially the initial ones, will take between 30 and 40 minutes. By understanding your funnels, you can make those minutes very productive.

Funnel Preparation — In each funnel, ask yourself "What are the five to ten points that I most want the interviewer to know about me?" Are you financing your own education? Is there a certain geographic area where you want to relocate? Should you make the interviewer aware of your grade-point average? What projects have you worked on during school? With what organizations are you involved? What leadership roles have you taken? Where have you performed well as a team member? When have you balanced several important projects at once? Do you have work experience related to the position for which you are applying?

Funnel Exercise #1

What points within each funnel would you want to emphasize to an interviewer? Once again, refer to your strengths and weaknesses on page 8, your Self-Inventory on pages 16-17, and "What Employers Look For" and "Why Employers Will Pay More" on page 18.

✎ PERSONAL BACKGROUND

Example: *"I'm financing 80 percent of my education expenses myself."*

_____
_____
_____
_____
_____
_____
_____

✎ EDUCATIONAL BACKGROUND

Example: *"My grade-point average is 3.5."*

_____
_____
_____
_____
_____
_____
_____

✏ ACTIVITIES AND ORGANIZATIONS

Example: *"I'm currently serving as vice president of the school's Marketing Club."*

_____
_____
_____
_____
_____
_____
_____

✏ WORK EXPERIENCE

Example: *"I currently work 30 hours per week as a shift leader at a local grocery store to help finance my education."*

_____
_____
_____
_____
_____
_____
_____

✏ CAREER GOALS

Example: *"One of my goals is to gain international experience and live abroad for some period of time."*

_____
_____
_____
_____
_____
_____
_____

In any interview, there is a series of questions that may cause the candidate to panic. I am referring to the dreaded "What would you say are your major weaknesses?" Or the equally dreaded "Has there been any time that you have failed or have not been as successful as you would have liked?" The interviewer will cringe if you say, "No, not really. I've never failed at anything in my life." The purpose of this question is to see how you have dealt with the adversity, not to exploit your failure.

You need to be honest with yourself about what questions you most fear. Hoping they won't be asked is sure to hurt your interviewing chances. Even if the question is not asked, you will not be as confident as you need to be. In the back of your mind, you will be anticipating the dreaded questions. This will show as a lack of confidence, and possibly, a lack of focus.

During many of my seminars, I ask what potential interview questions students most fear. At or near the top of the list is any question related to how long it has taken them to graduate. Students perceive taking longer than "normal" to graduate as a major stumbling block to impressing an interviewer.

Let's look at the facts behind employers' feelings toward this issue. The overwhelming majority of employers do not care if it has taken a student more than four years to graduate. According to a recent survey, only 17.2 percent of employers view graduating in four years as a strong positive. The majority of employers view it as somewhat positive (21.9 percent) or as neither positive nor negative (59.4 percent.) Completing a degree in five years is viewed as a neutral to 76.6 percent of employers with 14.1 percent categorizing it as either a strong, or somewhat strong positive influence. Only 9.4 percent of employers view this as a negative!

What employers do care about is *why*. Did you need to work? Did you change majors? Did you double major? Did you study abroad? Was there a family crisis? Most importantly, how did you come back from any adversity?

Very rarely will your biggest fear be relevant to the employer. What is a major concern to you may not even be a passing thought to the employer; however, if you do not prepare to discuss how you have handled adversity, your fears may sabotage the entire interview.

Product Knowledge

If an area of your background is a concern to the interviewer, preparation will help you to address the issue.

Also, how you have overcome your "failures" can impress the interviewer and set you apart. The bottom line is that preparation breeds confidence, and confidence dramatically increases your chances for success

✎ For the next exercise, within each funnel isolate the points that would cause you the most concern if asked by an interviewer. Then prepare an upbeat and positive response to those questions. For example, an individual who is carrying a 2.1 GPA might want to let the interviewer know that he is also working nearly full-time, while serving as treasurer of the engineering club.

Funnel Exercise #2

What three topics might be discussed during an interview that would cause you concern? How would you positively respond?

✏ PERSONAL BACKGROUND

Point: *"You are not geographically mobile?"*
Response: *"At least not initially. I am involved in the Big Sisters program, and want to live locally for at least the next two years, or until my little sister goes to high school."*

1. Point: _____
   _____
   _____

   Response: _____
   _____
   _____

2. Point: _____
   _____
   _____

   Response: _____
   _____
   _____

3. Point: _____
   _____
   _____

   Response: _____
   _____
   _____

EDUCATIONAL BACKGROUND

Point: *"Your GPA is only 2.1."*
Response: *"I have been extremely active in many campus activities. This has made it difficult to study as much as I'd like. However, I have established priorities for my time, and am maintaining a 3.5 GPA in my major."*

1. Point: _____

   Response: _____

2. Point: _____

   Response: _____

3. Point: _____

   Response: _____

✎ ACTIVITIES AND ORGANIZATIONS

Point: *"You are not involved in any on-campus activities."*
Response: *"As a commuting student who works 30 hours per week to finance my education, I've had little time for on-campus activities. When I do have extra time, I devote it to serving as a volunteer fire fighter."*

1. Point: _____
   _____
   _____

   Response: _____
   _____
   _____

2. Point: _____
   _____
   _____

   Response: _____
   _____
   _____

3. Point: _____
   _____
   _____

   Response: _____
   _____
   _____

WORK EXPERIENCE

Point: *"You have no real practical hands-on experience in marketing."*
Response: *"While I've not yet had an opportunity to actually work in a marketing environment, I am an active member of the marketing club. Also, I will be participating in an unpaid marketing internship later this semester at ABC Corporation."*

1. Point: _____

    Response: _____

2. Point: _____

    Response: _____

3. Point: _____

    Response: _____

✏ CAREER GOALS

Point: *"You've changed your major from chemistry to business management, which will require you to take an extra year to graduate."*

Response: *"While I planned to study science, I found out when I became vice president of the science club that I excelled at managing and directing people. Therefore, even though it will require an extra year of course work, I know I'll be more productive in my career."*

1. Point: _____

   Response: _____

2. Point: _____

   Response: _____

3. Point: _____

   Response: _____

✏ The following pages contain examples of funnels. After each example, place your area of most concern from funnel exercise #2 in the middle. By placing this in the middle, you can confidently explain how you learned from this "failure" and were able to overcome it and move on.

Example of How Your Funnels Work

The examples show:

1. The points you will want to share with an interviewer. Refer to pages 8, 16-17 and 18 to help your thought process.

2. The areas you are most concerned about ("failure") and how to place those concerns in the middle of your funnel.

3. Experiences from which you have learned, and how you overcame your "failures." Refer to the sample interview questions on page 30. Create a funnel for each "failure," addressing how you overcame the adversity.

4. Other important points you will want to share with an interviewer.

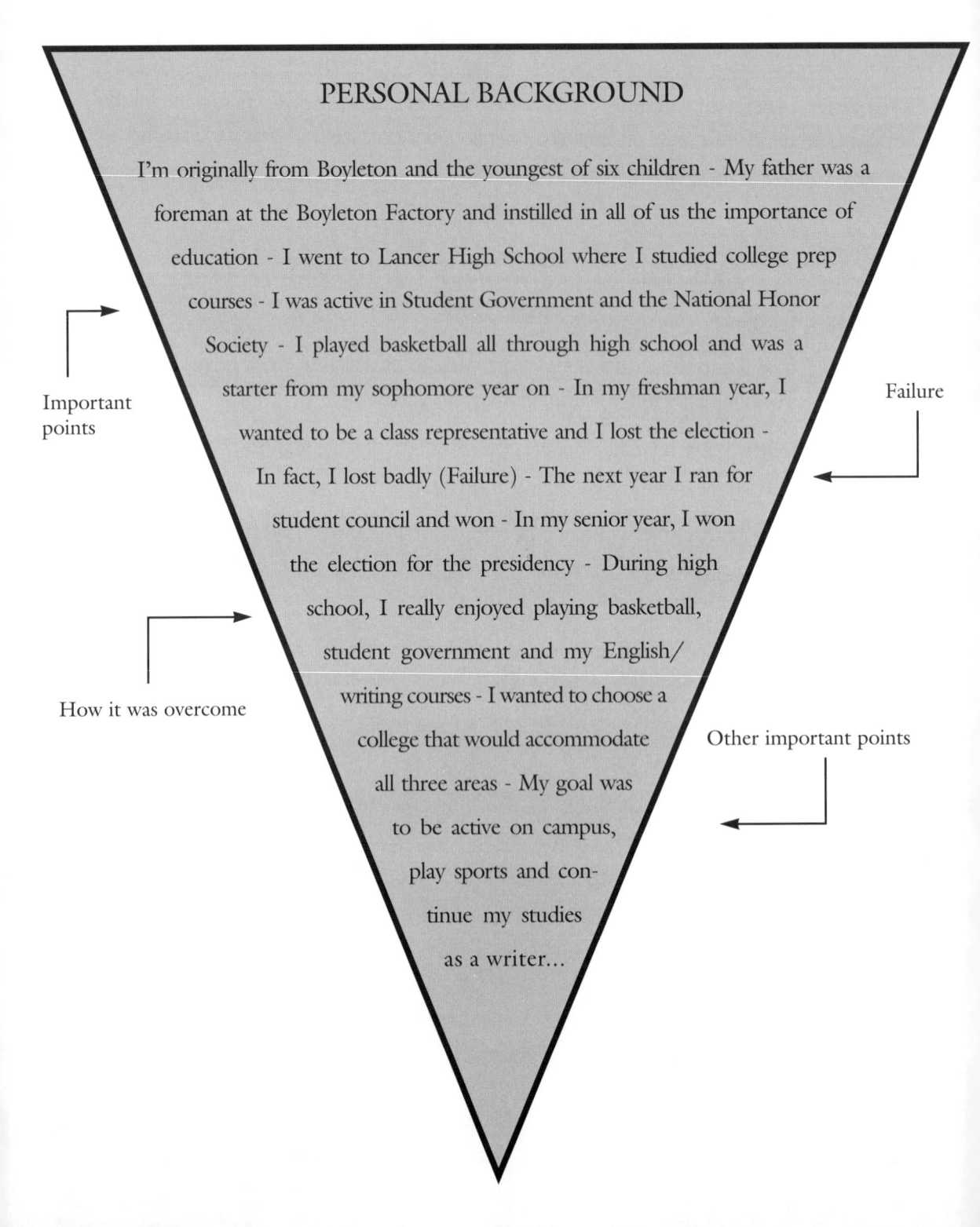

PERSONAL BACKGROUND

I'm originally from Boyleton and the youngest of six children - My father was a foreman at the Boyleton Factory and instilled in all of us the importance of education - I went to Lancer High School where I studied college prep courses - I was active in Student Government and the National Honor Society - I played basketball all through high school and was a starter from my sophomore year on - In my freshman year, I wanted to be a class representative and I lost the election - In fact, I lost badly (Failure) - The next year I ran for student council and won - In my senior year, I won the election for the presidency - During high school, I really enjoyed playing basketball, student government and my English/writing courses - I wanted to choose a college that would accommodate all three areas - My goal was to be active on campus, play sports and continue my studies as a writer...

Important points

Failure

How it was overcome

Other important points

PERSONAL BACKGROUND

Important points

Failure

How it was overcome

Other important points

PERSONAL BACKGROUND

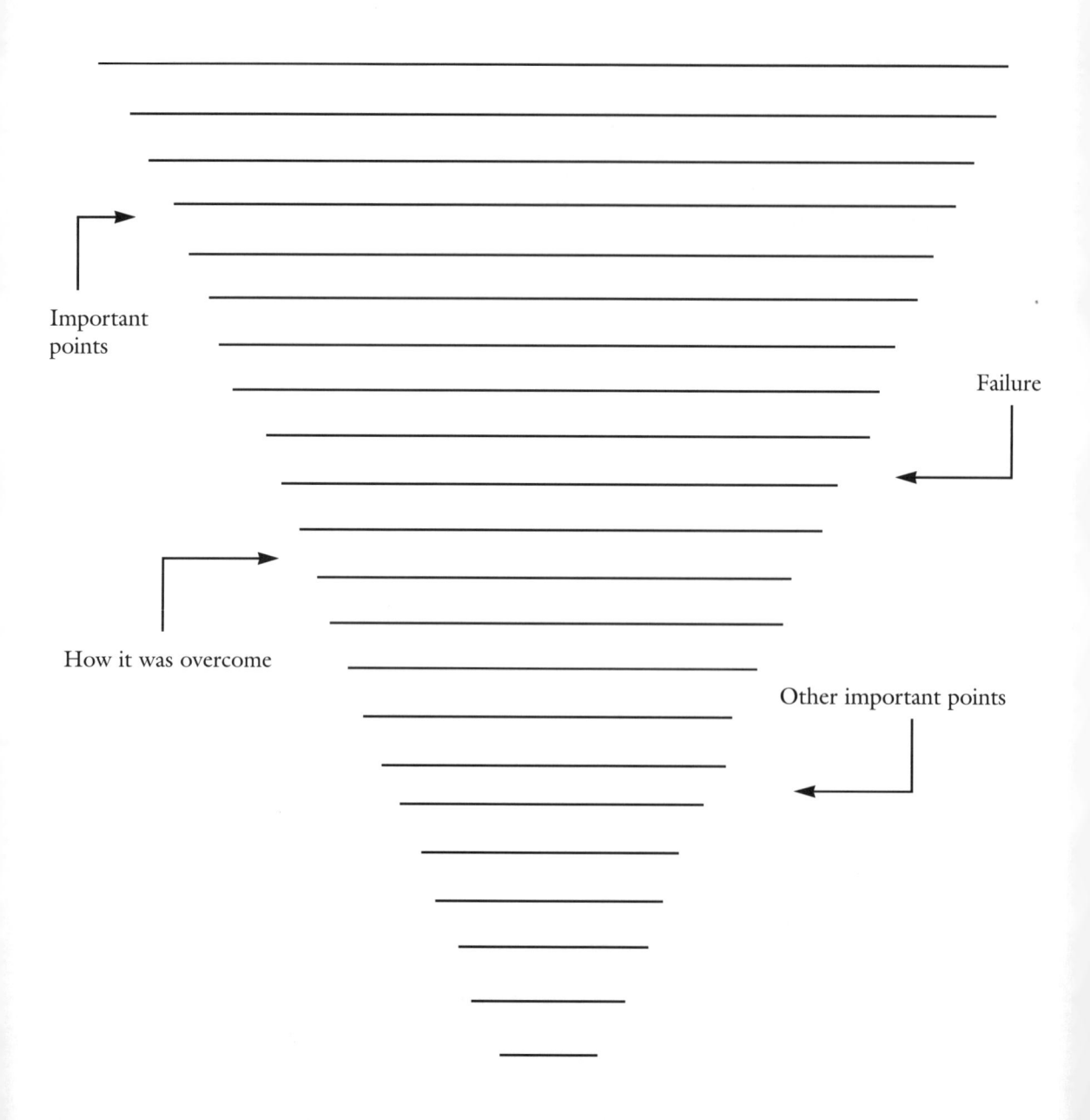

Important points

How it was overcome

Failure

Other important points

PERSONAL BACKGROUND

Important points →

Failure ←

How it was overcome →

Other important points ←

EDUCATIONAL BACKGROUND

I chose Central Main University because I originally wanted to pursue a writing career - I also wanted to study political science and I felt Central Main was a good choice for both areas - I realized that writing was a significant part of all of my classes; however, I enjoyed political science and history more than writing - I switched my major to public policy and history - In my sophomore year, I did not handle the switch well and my GPA was 1.88 (Failure) - The next semester, I really focused on my studies and my new major - I guess I better learned how to prioritize and manage several projects at once - For the last two years, I have not earned less than a 3.2 - I made the Dean's List in my senior year - School has taught me a great deal about communication, project management and problem solving - These skills will help me as I pursue a career in...

Important points

Failure

How it was overcome

Other important points

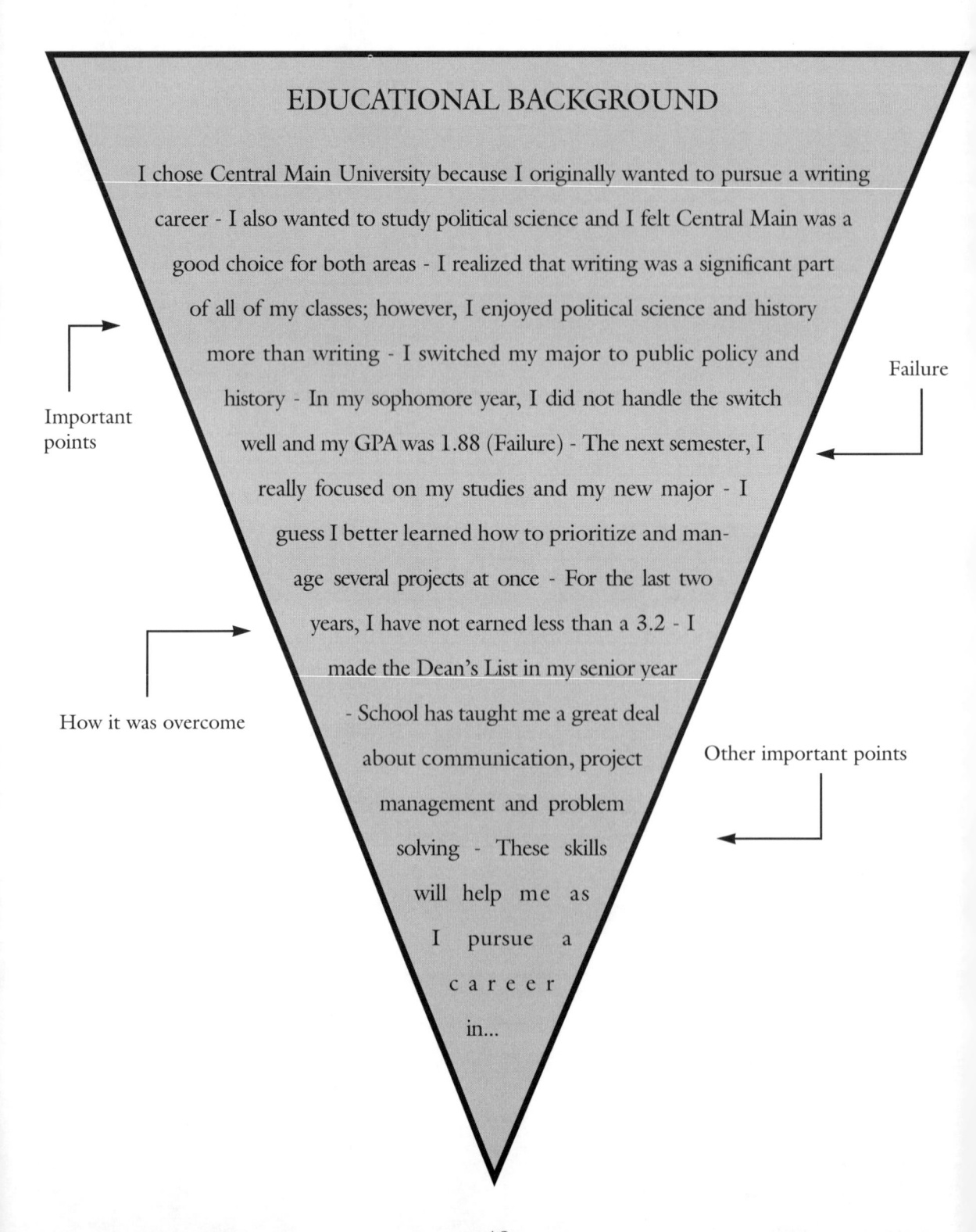

EDUCATIONAL BACKGROUND

Important points →

Failure ←

How it was overcome →

Other important points ←

49

EDUCATIONAL BACKGROUND

Important points →

Failure ←

How it was overcome →

Other important points ←

50

Product Knowledge

EDUCATIONAL BACKGROUND

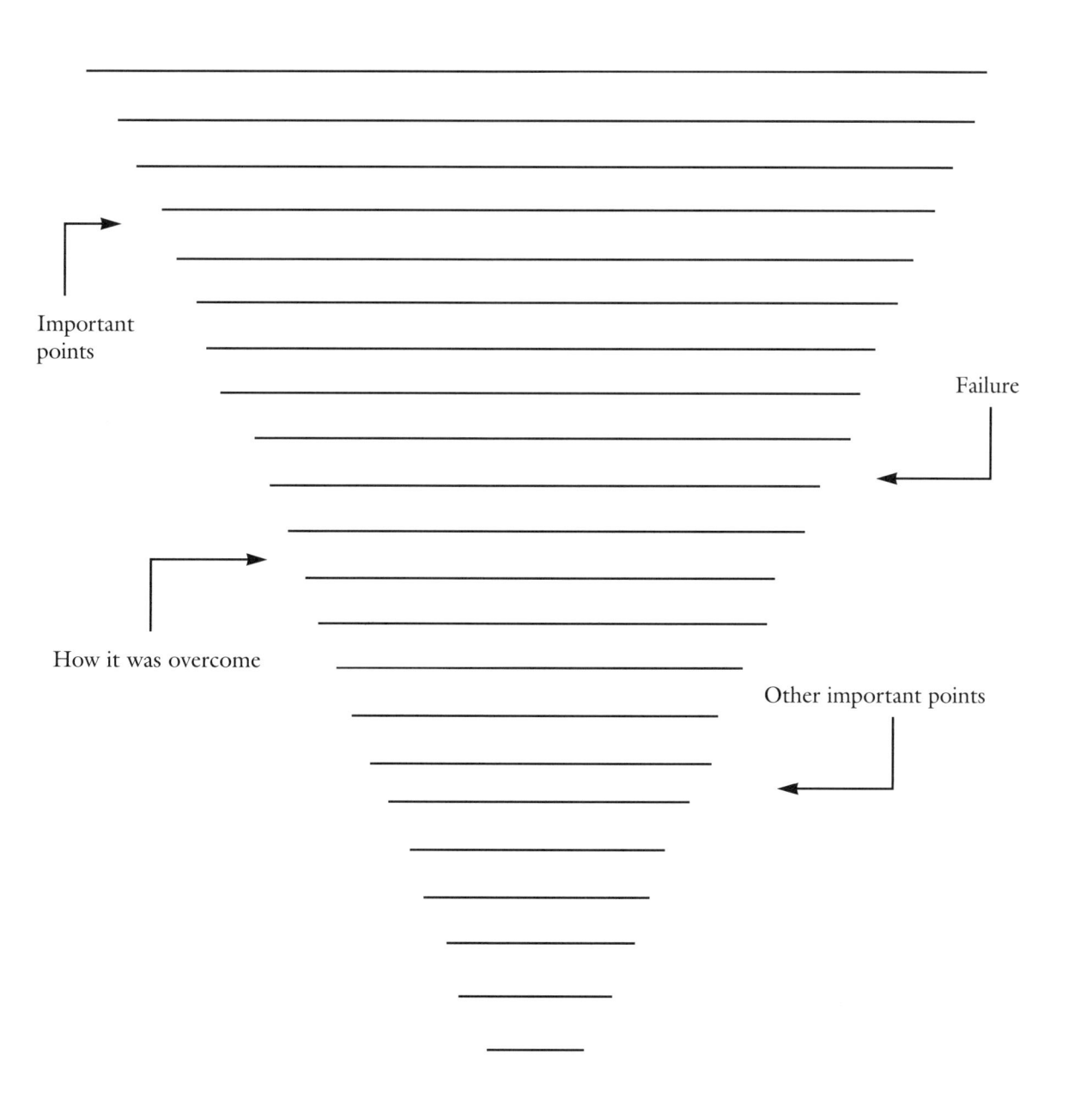

Important points →

Failure ←

How it was overcome →

Other important points ←

ACTIVITIES AND ORGANIZATIONS

In addition to my course of study, I chose Central Main because of my interest in student activities and also because I wanted to play basketball - I have been very active in the History Club - I lettered in basketball all four years and was elected captain in my senior year by the players and coaches - With the History Club, I chaired several committees and organized several successful events - One event I chaired was not at all successful - I tried to organize a reenactment of a Civil War battle during homecoming weekend - The turnout was very low and I was embarrassed to showcase the History Club with such a poorly-attended event (Failure) - The following year we tried again and expanded our team and advertising efforts - I tried to learn from my mistakes and make the necessary adjustments - The event went off without a hitch and was one of the more popular events - The activities I participated in have helped me to balance several different priorities at once - Also, I am learning valuable teamwork and leadership skills, which will help me in my career...

Important points

Failure

How it was overcome

Other important points

ACTIVITIES AND ORGANIZATIONS

Important points

Failure

How it was overcome

Other important points

ACTIVITIES AND ORGANIZATIONS

Important points

Failure

How it was overcome

Other important points

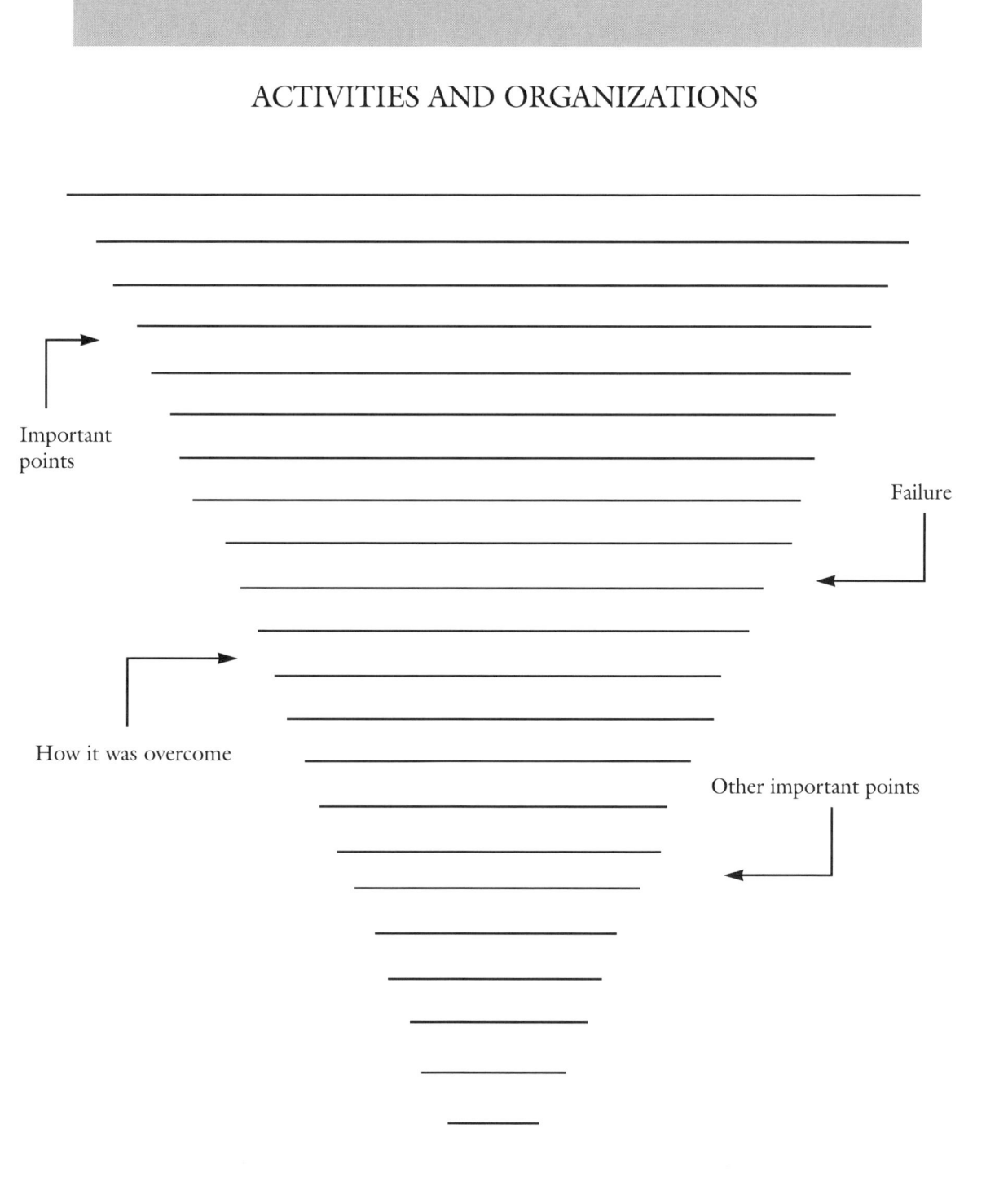

ACTIVITIES AND ORGANIZATIONS

Important points

Failure

How it was overcome

Other important points

WORK EXPERIENCE

I have always worked in some type of job - When I was eight years old, I took a paper route and expanded it from 30 to 45 houses - I didn't give up the route until I was old enough to get another job - Most of my summer jobs were to make enough money for school - I am financing 100 percent of my education and my first work priority has been to earn enough to pay my tuition - I applied for a job at the Boyleton factory my freshman year and didn't get hired (Failure) - I worked two jobs that summer in order to pay for school - The next summer I applied again, only this time in person, and was hired - I have been working in the factory every summer since, which allows me to save enough for my tuition - In order to pay for room and board, I work 20 hours per week for the intramural department as the equipment manager - This job has taught me how to interact with different types of people and how to stay organized - My work experience has taught me how to focus and break down tasks into more manageable pieces in order to reach my goals - As a result of my work experience, I will graduate on time and...

Important points

Failure

How it was overcome

Other important points

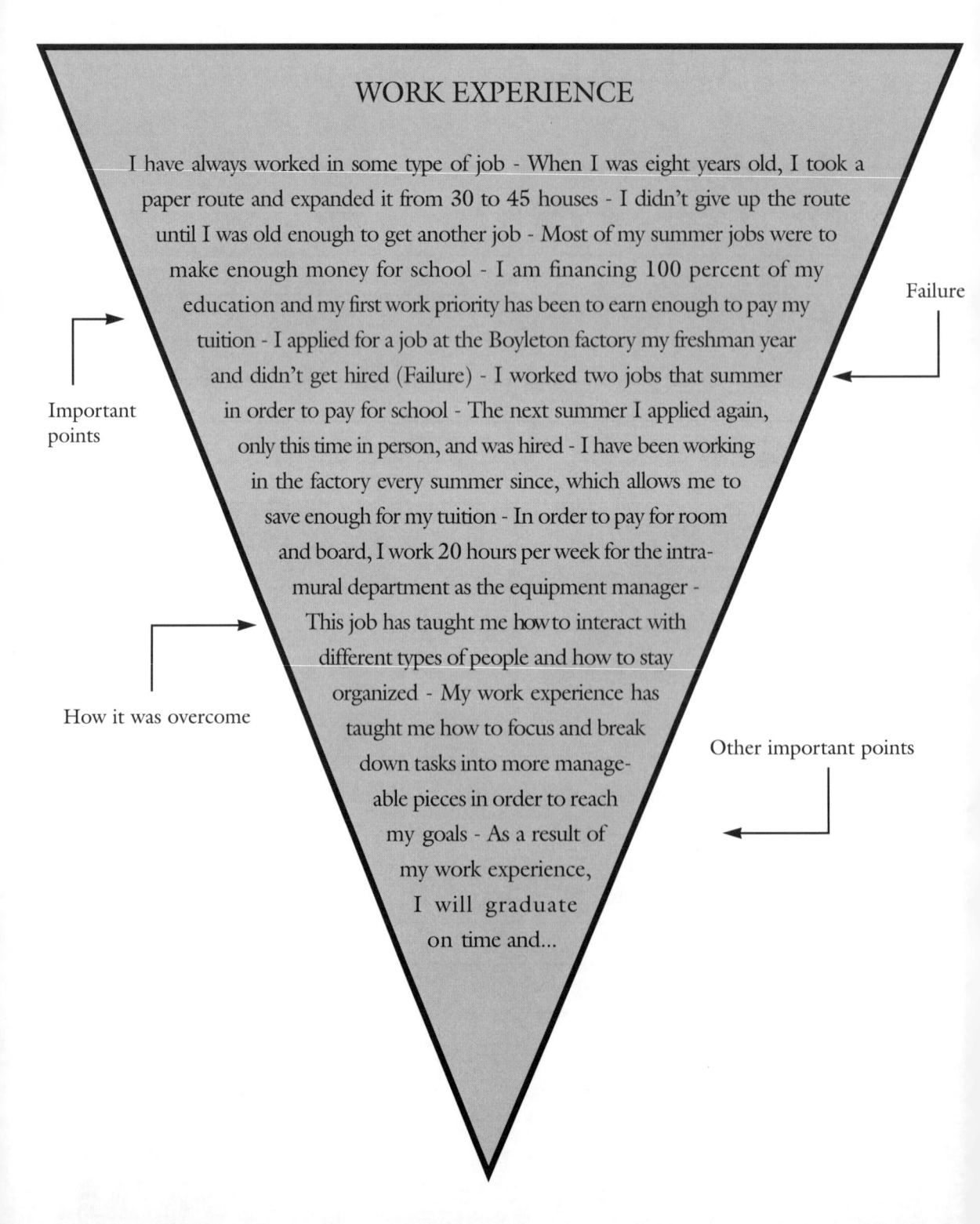

Product Knowledge

WORK EXPERIENCE

Important points

Failure

How it was overcome

Other important points

WORK EXPERIENCE

Important points

Failure

How it was overcome

Other important points

WORK EXPERIENCE

Important points

Failure

How it was overcome

Other important points

CAREER GOALS

I have decided to pursue a career in sales - I enjoy leading and motivating others and would ultimately like to move into a management position - I want to get into sales because I enjoy a challenge and have always taken responsibility for my performance, whether it was in school, basketball or the History Club - Sales holds an individual responsible for his or her performance - Success is in his or her hands - I do not have any practical sales and marketing experience - I had applied for an internship in the Boyleton marketing department, but I didn't get the job (Failure) - In order to gain as much experience as possible I tried to work on all of the sales and marketing assignments in the History Club - The second Civil War reenactment gave me a great opportunity to sell our program to both the local business and student/alumni communities - I also enjoy working on a team and would like to lead a sales team some day in the near future...

Important points

Failure

How it was overcome

Other important points

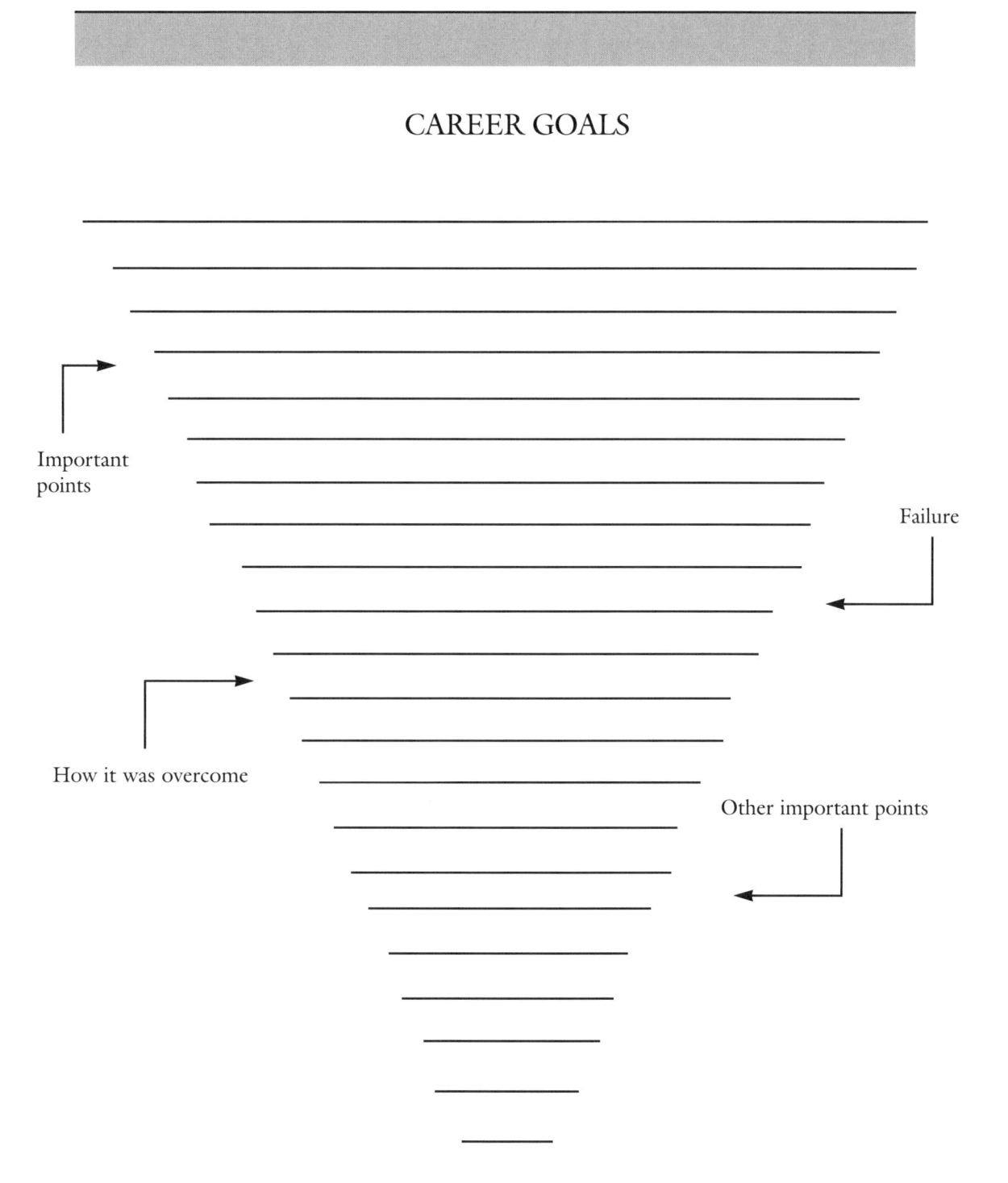

CAREER GOALS

Important points →

Failure ←

How it was overcome →

Other important points ←

CAREER GOALS

Important points

Failure

How it was overcome

Other important points

CAREER GOALS

Important points

Failure

How it was overcome

Other important points

Practice

The interviewing process can be nerve-wracking. Everyone's palms are sweaty when they first begin interviewing. Recently a friend of mine was interviewing for the first time in his career since college. Even though he had an extraordinary track record, there were several areas in his funnels where he lacked confidence. He believed his background was not adequate for the position. Also, he felt uncomfortable with a few other areas of his résumé, namely the lack of community activities.

The concerns he had about his background, despite his track record, actually had caused him to turn down other opportunities in the past. Realizing a need to further his career, this time he was determined to market himself effectively.

We worked together, and he listed the points he would most fear being brought up in an interview. Next, he listed several responses to each point and practiced each response several times, even agreeing to be "grilled" with the "failure" questions.

His preparation complete, he began interviewing. After two interviews, he had received two job offers, finally accepting a position with one of the world's largest corporations. He believes that his success came from identifying his areas of concern and preparing in advance. "No one likes to interview, even if you have been working for years," he told me afterward. "Taking the time to prepare my funnels, however, gave me a sense of confidence about the interview process. While I have had a few missteps, my résumé and experience were perfect for the job and the company.

"Since I was prepared for the process, I entered each session with a sense of purpose that I'm sure came through to the interviewer. My confidence, through preparation, allowed for a more productive session. Not only was I more relaxed and natural, I also thought the interviewer was more open."

By taking the time to prepare and study your funnels, you will not be eliminating your nervousness. What you will be doing is eliminating all of the negative thoughts associated with the interviewing process. If not prepared, everyone worries about:

- What questions are going to be asked?
- What kinds of questions should I ask?
- What if I freeze up?
- What if my nervousness shows?
- What if they ask…?

Practicing the presentation of each funnel will provide you with a "talk track" to follow during the interview. Regardless of what questions are asked in the session, you will be prepared to direct the conversation toward your strengths.

Whether you are sitting with a seasoned interviewer or a novice, the funnel concept will provide you with the necessary tools to excel. Remember how you have felt during tests. While you may always be nervous, knowing that you are prepared is comforting.

Once you have completed all of your funnels, practice each one individually. This will help to let the information flow naturally. Read aloud your personal background funnel into a tape recorder. Play it back and make any changes you find necessary. Do this until you are satisfied that the words are flowing smoothly. Then repeat the process for each funnel.

After you have refined the wording, begin practicing each funnel without your notes. Start with your personal background funnel and stick with it until you can smoothly work your way through the entire funnel. Then move on to the next funnel and practice it in the same manner.

Do not short-cut your practice efforts. You must be able to present each area confidently. As you become more comfortable with all of your funnels, begin to move back and forth from funnel to funnel. This will be helpful should you find yourself in an unstructured interview.

Another practice suggestion is to work on your funnel presentations with someone else. Have your partner throw out the "failure question" from each funnel and record how smoothly you handled it. Take note of how you feel during your answers. At first you will be nervous and unsure of your responses. Do not step out of role-play. During a real interview you cannot call time out. Simply stumble your way through it and then try again. When your nervousness subsides, you will know that you are ready.

During your practice role-plays, do not "say what you're going to say" by paraphrasing your answer. Say it exactly as you would in an interview. The actual verbiage can then be adjusted. Paraphrasing will only give you a false sense of security; people seldom respond the way they think they will.

A final suggestion is to use a video camera. The video camera won't lie and will provide you with invaluable feedback. Working with someone else and using the camera also will help you to simulate an interview. There is something a bit nerve-wracking about being in front of a camera. Film yourself from several angles. You never see yourself from a side angle and this view will show you how others might be seeing you.

Creating and practicing your funnels will provide you with a competitive edge and increase your chances for success. Your competition may already have both interviewing and work experience. You can't create work experience, but you can overcome the lack of interviewing experience.

Checklist for Practicing Your Funnels

- [ ] Complete your funnels.

- [ ] Begin practicing one funnel at a time.

- [ ] Read aloud your "script" into a tape recorder. Make any necessary changes.

- [ ] Practice your funnel without your notes until you are comfortable.

- [ ] Go to the next funnel.

- [ ] Once you are confident that you know all of your funnels, begin to "bounce around."

- [ ] Practice with a friend.

- [ ] Have the friend ask the "failure" question.

- [ ] Do not "step out" of role-play.

- [ ] Do not paraphrase your answers. State them exactly as you would during an interview.

- [ ] Film yourself from three angles: front, right and left side.

Notes for *Product Knowledge:*

Notes for *Product Knowledge:*

> "It is not the will to win that makes a champion, everyone has that. It is the will to prepare to win that makes a champion."
>
> — Bobby Knight,
> legendary college basketball coach

Chapter 4

Market Knowledge

Creative Research

Now that you have created your brochure, and studied and practiced your product knowledge, it is time to develop an understanding of the market. If your product is going to be a success, and you're going to close that one multi-million-dollar sale, you must know your "target market."

Before every interview, you will need to research your prospective employer. The more you know, the more you will stand out from your competition. Setting yourself apart can be difficult, since every other job candidate likely will be reviewing the same information. Therefore, you will need to be resourceful in your research.

Challenge yourself to find new and creative ways to gather information about a prospective employer. You might be tempted to let this part of the process slide and to review some superficial information a few hours before the interview. Taking that approach will diminish your chances for success at a very critical point in your job search.

My friend Bob Perrin, a human resource expert, has a very strong opinion on this matter. During his career, he has interviewed thousands of candidates and filled a wide range of positions, from entry-level clerical jobs to those requiring advanced medical degrees.

"Most people research the obvious," Perrin points out. "Their idea of preparation is to read some basic information and memorize statistics and numbers. While this might be new information to them, I already know it. And worse, they will be the tenth person to recite it to me this week. At best, they have met, not exceeded, my expectations.

"The person who stands out the most is the one who goes beyond the obvious: the person who displays an interest in learning and who shows some problem-solving and analytical ability. It is not always easy to find information, but the person who does, already has proven to me both his desire and his problem-solving nature.

"For example, what is our mission statement and what are our strategies for achieving our goals?

Did you research any of our products and/or critically shop at one of our outlets? Did you take the time to check our Web page? How about the Web pages of our competitors? If you did, you can engage me in a much more interesting conversation.

"Don't quote statistics," Perrin advises. "It's too cold. Engage me in conversation about deeper, more conceptual issues. You can only do that with creative research."

As we discussed in Chapter 2, rightsizing and the competitive forces of the marketplace have severely limited the time available to most workers. This is also true for the interviewer. You can use this reality to your advantage. Again, allow me to bring you around to my side, the interviewer's side, of the desk. Interviewing is only one of the tasks I must do in my job. There are literally dozens of other functions I must perform.

Given all of my responsibilities, and because my time is at a premium, I am not able to digest all of the information that comes my way. Even if I had the time, the marketplace is changing so rapidly I would still not be able to keep up with the changes. I have come to realize how important knowledge is and how much I value knowledge resources. Anyone or anything that can provide me with quick access to useful information gets my attention.

Conversely, anyone who cannot provide me with information, or who imposes on my time to access basic information, will not get my attention. I value knowledge resources and I avoid knowledge drains. To get my time and attention, you need to be a resource. If you are prepared for an interview and have conducted some creative research, you have a much better chance of getting my attention and respect.

Several years ago, I received a call from a student who had attended one of my lectures. After completing her bachelor's degree, she had decided to attend law school and was about to graduate. She called me for a "refresher."

About a month later, she called again to follow up. She had just landed her dream job and wanted to thank me. As a young attorney, her competition was not just other recent graduates, but also experienced lawyers. By conducting creative research, she was able to gain an edge on this competition.

A local law firm was looking to add experienced associates, so she applied, in spite of the fact that she lacked the requisite experience. Prior to her initial interview, she began to research the firm. What she discovered was that 28 percent of the firm's business was generated by two large clients based in Italy.

Her résumé did not show any language skills because she had never taken a formal course. But both of her grandparents spoke only Italian, and she had learned to speak it fluently. If she had not done the research, she never would have known to bring this up during the interview. Even though she lacked the experience, she landed the job and is a full partner today. I asked her how she discovered the Italian clients. Her answer was brilliant in its simplicity: "I called and asked the receptionist who their largest clients were, then I researched their clients' businesses."

Law firms, like other privately held businesses, may not publish annual reports and other similar materials — the typical standby information for those preparing for interviews. So, a bit of creativity and problem solving will go a long way. The interviewer most likely will be impressed with your efforts. If you do your homework and still do not find any useful information, let the interviewer know what you did do to research the company.

⌛ How can you set yourself apart? A lot of that answer lies within you. How have you set yourself apart in the past? In every step of your job search, you will need to access your courage and bring your own individuality into the process. *You are a unique product.*

How did you manage your overloaded class schedule? How did you go about studying for two tests at the same time? How were you able to find "just the right article" for that term paper? These questions, and similar ones, will help you tap into your own creative research abilities.

There are hundreds of ways to do market research. Your placement office will have a great deal of information on prospective employers, including information beyond annual reports and recent quarterly reports. Many companies will furnish your placement office with volumes of valuable information. Therefore, the placement office is a good place to start.

As you prepare to interview, come up with other creative ways to understand the market. It is never too early to begin your search for information. Take advantage of every opportunity to become a knowledge resource.

For your next gift to yourself, purchase a share of stock in a prospective employer. If you have always wanted to work for an automobile manufacturer, why not buy, or have someone buy for you, a share of stock in one.

This share of stock will give you access to an incredible amount of information about the automobile industry. You will receive all of the material published for shareholders. You'll gain access to valuable information about the company, as well as its competitors and the industry in general. A share of stock in any company will keep you informed about that company's industry. You don't need to purchase the most expensive stock available. The stock market lists hundreds of companies with affordable stock prices.

As a stockholder, you will be an owner of the company. The information you receive as an owner, and your analysis of this information, will give you a distinct advantage during an interview. You will be able to tailor your funnels to a particular industry and to formulate solid, intelligent questions.

✎ The following exercise will help you develop creative ways to research a company.

Creative Research

In what industry or company have you chosen to pursue a career, and what position do you want to obtain?

Industry/Company:_____
Position:_____

What questions can you ask about the industry or company?

? _____
? _____
? _____
? _____
? _____

Market Knowledge

Sample questions:

- What product does the company produce?
- What is its mode of distribution?
- Have I used the product/service? What are my impressions of it?
- Do I know people who have used the product/service? What are their impressions?
- What can I learn about their competition?

How can you creatively research the industry or company to exceed the interviewer's expectations?

? _____
? _____
? _____
? _____
? _____

Sample creative research ideas:

- Buy a share of stock in the company.
- Buy a share of stock in a competitor.
- Shop the company's stores.
- Review the company's Web site, and the sites of its competitors.
- Talk to current employees.
- Look in magazines for recent articles on the company.
- Look in magazines for recent articles on the company's competitors.
- Look in magazines for recent articles on the company's customers.

Examples:

Industry: Sales
Position: Management Trainee
Research: Call a local firm and ask to speak to a salesperson. Explain your purpose to the salesperson and interview him/her for a few minutes.

Industry: Electronics
Position: Customer Service Representative
Research: Talk to a current user of the product (or similar products) to better understand what is expected from someone in this position.

Industry: Education
Position: School Teacher
Research: Attend PTA meetings and talk to parents. Attend a school board meeting.

Industry: Retail
Position: Assistant Buyer
Research: Walk through several store locations as well as competing stores. Take a notebook and record your observations.

Industry: High Technology
Position: Market Analyst
Research: Using the Internet, locate information about the company and a few of its competitors.

Industry: _____
Position: _____
Research: _____
_____
_____

Industry: _____
Position: _____
Research: _____
_____
_____

Industry: _____
Position: _____
Research: _____
_____
_____

Industry: _____
Position: _____
Research: _____
_____
_____

Industry: _____
Position: _____
Research: _____
_____
_____

Industry: _____
Position: _____
Research: _____
_____
_____
_____

Industry: _____
Position: _____
Research: _____
_____
_____
_____

Industry: _____
Position: _____
Research: _____
_____
_____
_____

Industry: _____
Position: _____
Research: _____
_____
_____
_____

Industry: _____
Position: _____
Research: _____
_____
_____
_____

Refer again to page 8 where you outlined your strengths and weaknesses. What did you list as your strengths? How can you tap into these strengths to creatively research a prospective company? Look at your first strength. What does it tell you about conducting market research? You do have the courage to be different.

There are many ways in which researching a company may, at first, be uncomfortable. For example, calling a prospective employer and asking to talk to an employee in a similar position might seem hard; however, you will find the hardest part is dialing the phone. People love to help and they will be impressed that you called. Ask what he likes and dislikes about the job. How did she obtain the position? Be aggressive, professional, and respect this person's time. If you need to, set a phone appointment and call back. Your efforts may impress the employee so much that he or she may mention it to the interviewer. If so, you will already be one step ahead of your competition.

Communication Skills

Once you have completed your research and funnels, you will need to present this knowledge in a clear, concise, and persuasive manner. Therefore, you must understand what communication skills the market demands.

In the interviewing process, there are three major areas of communication:

1. Telephone skills
2. Letter-writing
3. Face-to-face meetings[*]

Each is equally important. An impression is formed during all communications. Have you ever talked to someone on the telephone whom you haven't met? Did you draw a conclusion about this person from their voice, grammar, vocabulary, and conversation style? In fact, haven't you "drawn a picture in your mind" of what this person looks like? If you had the chance to meet him or her, would you compare your "mental picture" with the real thing?

---

[*] In Chapter 6, face-to-face communication will be discussed further as it pertains to the actual interview.

When communicating with a prospective employer on the telephone, these same processes are occurring. The person on the other end of the line is drawing a mental picture. This picture will be either positive or negative. If negative, you may never have the chance to overcome it in a face-to-face meeting.

Some of the biggest mistakes made during the job search are made over the telephone. Too often you want to hide behind the telephone and, because it is not a face-to-face meeting, you feel safe.

DO NOT FALL INTO THIS TRAP! When you are sitting down to call a prospective employer, make sure that you are mentally prepared. How do you want the conversation to go? What are your objectives for the conversation? Write them down. In other words, visualize the ideal outcome of the telephone call, and set that as your objective. If you do not set an objective for the telephone call, how will you know if it has been a successful interaction?

Once you have set your objectives, outline the conversation to reach your objective. This may be as simple as confirming an interview time or as complicated as trying to sell yourself to get the first interview. Either way, you need to outline the steps necessary to accomplish your objective.

The following exercise will help you sharpen your telephone skills.

Developing Your Telephone Skills

For the following exercise, you must:

1. Prepare a concise introduction of yourself.
2. Decide what your objectives are for the call.
3. Practice the call.

1. Prepare your introduction.

Example: "Hello, my name is Brian Drake and I am graduating from Central Main University in May."

Hello, _____
_____

2. List your objectives.

Example: Objective: To get an appointment.
Objective: To confirm the time and date of an appointment.
Objective: To find out with whom you will be meeting.

Objective: _____
Objective: _____
Objective: _____

3. Script the entire message and practice.

Example: "Hello, Ms. Roberts, my name is Brian Drake and I am graduating from Central Main University in May. I understand that you are interviewing for the position of sales trainee. I would like to confirm my appointment for March 5 at 9 a.m. (If this is left in voice mail, add, "If nothing has changed I will see you on the 5th, otherwise please call me at 555-2121. Thank you.")

_____
_____
_____

1. Prepare your introduction.

Hello,
_____
_____

2. List your objectives.

Objective: _____
Objective: _____
Objective: _____

3. Script the entire message and practice.

_____
_____
_____
_____
_____
_____
_____
_____
_____
_____
_____
_____
_____

1. Prepare your introduction.

Hello,
_____
_____

2. List your objectives.

Objective: _____
Objective: _____
Objective: _____

3. Script the entire message and practice.

_____
_____
_____
_____
_____
_____
_____
_____
_____
_____
_____
_____
_____

When you sit down to make the telephone call, clear your work area of all distractions. Pick up the telephone and practice asking for the person and walking him or her through your end of the conversation using your script. Make sure you are in the right frame of mind. Be prepared to be upbeat and positive. Do not make the telephone call and try to "fake it," believing that the other person will not be forming an impression of you since he or she cannot see you.

When using the telephone, be prepared to get your point across via voice mail. Voice mail has become a reality in most organizations. Often an unprepared person will reach voice mail and stutter and stammer. Being unprepared and leaving a long-winded, choppy message presents a negative image. Such a message says the caller does not respect my time and will waste my time even further if I were to meet him or her face-to-face.

Your voice mail message should be spoken clearly, but not like a robot. Always leave a return number and a good time to be reached. Do not ask for a return call unless something has changed (see example). By remembering these points, you will demonstrate your respect for efficiency and eliminate "phone tag." Practice your "voice mail voice" into a tape recorder. Concentrate on being natural and do not rush through the return phone number.

If you are sitting down to make several "prospecting" telephone calls to potential employers or people from your network, it is even more critical that you are thoroughly prepared. Each telephone call should be reviewed in advance. For every contact made, have your objectives and a conversational script prepared in advance.

Now, I am going to give you one piece of "backward" advice. If you have 10 people to telephone, and two or three of them are the highest priority, I recommend that you go through the list "backwards." Begin by calling the tenth most important person first. You may have been taught to target the highest priority first. When it comes to placing these phone calls, run that philosophy in reverse.

By starting with your tenth most important person, you will uncover all of your areas for improvement and gain significant practice while whittling away the list to get to your most important calls. When you reach the last call, or your number one priority, you will have made all of your mistakes. Since you will be correcting all of these mistakes along the way, you will be better prepared for your top priority.

The second area of communication that should not be taken for granted is letter-writing. Since it is not a face-to-face meeting, you sometimes feel safer communicating in writing. If you feel more comfortable, you may tend to let down your guard and not present yourself as positively or professionally as possible. But don't be fooled — perceptions about you are being formed by the person reading your written word.

Take advantage of your resources and ask your professors and the counselors in your placement office for help. Each of these people will be more than happy to help with your letters of introduction, follow-up/thank-you letters and any other business correspondence. To tide you over until you can get to the placement office or your appointment with a professor, there are a few samples in the next two chapters.

The third and final form of communication is the face-to-face meeting. Such a meeting typically falls into one of two categories: 1) you take it for granted; or 2) you dread it.

Those people who tend to easily interact with others often will take a face-to-face meeting too lightly. Others, meanwhile, who find it difficult to socialize, will nervously dread meeting new people. Either approach can be very destructive to your job search.

There is a third way to categorize a face-to-face meeting: as an outgrowth of all the preparation for your job search. You feel confident about your product and are clear about your objective for each meeting. Therefore, each of your face-to-face contacts needs to be viewed as a "focused interaction," not a casual meeting or a dreaded interview.

During your job search, not all of your face-to-face meetings will be formal interviews. Much of the personal contact you have will be in a more casual atmosphere. We will discuss these meetings in more detail later on.

Notes for *Market Knowledge:*

Notes for *Market Knowledge:*

> *"A wise man will make more opportunities than he finds."*
>
> — Francis Bacon,
> seventeenth-century English philosopher

Chapter 5

Prospecting

Identifying Potential Employers

For years, sales people have referred to the initial stage of the sales cycle as "prospecting." Prospects are *potential* customers. Once a prospect is identified, a strategy is put into place to advance the sale.

As you begin your job search, you will need to focus on generating prospects. Prospects would include direct job opportunities or people who can lead you to opportunities. In either case, you need to take a broad view of your world and begin to search for prospects.

The place to start your search is at your school's placement office. Many businesses use college placement offices as a primary tool for finding entry-level employees. If you haven't done so already, make an appointment to meet with someone in your school's office as soon as possible.

In addition to your placement office, there are several other resources to explore. One of the fastest growing sources of opportunities is the Internet. Many organizations are using the Internet to post job openings and to source applicants, and are publicizing their home page addresses to college placement offices.

Familiarity with the Internet is fast becoming a necessity for graduating students. Companies find that advertising on-line is far less expensive than placing classified ads. Also, when utilizing the Internet, a direct link can be established between the candidate and the company. *Be prepared to e-mail your résumé to a prospective employer!*

Despite the emergence of the Internet, traditional, low-tech resources should not be overlooked. Newspapers are still a great source. Begin as soon as possible to scour the "help wanted" section of your local newspaper. Also, do not hesitate to send your résumé to a company you see advertising in the paper *even if the advertised position is not in your field*. While an organization may advertise for specific positions, it may not for others. That does not mean it isn't hiring people with your qualifications. You may well increase your chances of getting an interview in your field, since your competition may have overlooked this opportunity.

A help-wanted ad may include a great deal of useful information. To illustrate, look at the following example:

> **Advertising**
> **Creative Assistant**
> Fast-paced, growing firm dedicated to excellence is looking for a Creative Assistant with a B.A. degree in advertising and a minimum of six months experience, to assist Director. Responsibilities to include: client interaction, project management, copy design, presentation preparation. Send résumé to: XYZ Company, PO Box 2121, Mifflinwood, USA 11111 ATTN: VALERIE or e-mail to:www.xyzadvertise.com
> **XYZ Company**
> • Our mission is excellence •

Prospecting Sources[6]
On-line

- Job Choices
- Jobnet
- Jobwire
- On-line Career Fairs

- E-Span
- Monster Board
- JobTrak

Other

- Local newspaper ads
- National newspaper ads*
- Faculty referrals
- Staff referrals
- Campus publications
- Placement firms

- Career fairs
- Letters sent directly to employers
- Student organizations
- Trade publications
- Community agencies
- Professional journals

* Have a relative, friend or contact send you the paper from your target cities.

[6] L. Patrick Sheetz, Ph.D., Recruiting Trends 1996-97, 26th ed., (Michigan State University: Michigan, 1996).

Prospecting for your first job is going to require some effort on your part. The key is to *keep your eyes and ears open*. Job opportunities sometimes pop up in the strangest places. Sometimes all you have to do is ask. Do not just talk to people you come in regular contact with; ask everyone who might hear of an opportunity.

A few years ago, a colleague of mine who owns several successful businesses decided to open an upscale restaurant and conference center. In order to attract his target customers he chose a very high-profile location and set out to hire the best work force available. He decided to engage a search firm to fill all of the key positions. After several weeks, a "world class" team of professionals, recruited from around the country, was assembled. A few days before the grand opening, his food and beverage manager resigned. At this point, there was no time to conduct another extensive search, so the decision was made to move ahead with all of the original plans.

Almost immediately, things began to falter. The departed manager had not attended to dozens of key tasks and morale was low among the other managers who were having to pick up the slack. The grand opening was in jeopardy.

My colleague happened to stop in at his local bank, and the teller, who knew about his plans for the new restaurant, asked how things were going. In a moment of frustration, he told her of the problems he was having since the loss of the manager.

After listening politely, the teller asked if he minded taking a call from another customer, a recent graduate with a hotel management degree. The recent graduate had made everyone she knew aware of her job search. A bank, the graduate reasoned, deals with many local businesses and might be a good source of referrals.

My friend met the recent grad and hired her on the spot. In order to prove herself, she worked extraordinarily hard to catch up, even taking a heavy workload home at night. To this day, my friend is not sure if he hired her out of desperation or because he admired the aggressive way she went about prospecting for a job opportunity. Today she is the general manager, directing the entire restaurant operation. Her "search firm" was the local bank teller.

Networking

You have probably heard about the "hidden job market" and how most job vacancies are never advertised in the papers. Fortunately, this is true. I say "fortunately" because once you learn how to uncover these opportunities, you will have less competition. "Networking" is the tool that will help you learn about the hidden opportunities.

Networking is, quite simply, friend building, but many view it in rather negative terms.

Not long ago, I conducted a networking seminar at a prestigious university. Following the talk, a student approached me and asked, "Isn't networking just a nice word for using people?" The student was from India and had been told that, in addition to getting a great education in the United States, he would also meet many contacts. The concept of "making contacts" made him uncomfortable.

My answer to him was, "What if we substituted the word 'contacts' with the word 'friends'?" Then I asked, "How do you feel about making friends?"

He said he had made many friends while in school. In fact, he intended to stay in touch with many of his classmates after graduation. "But," he said, "I could never 'use them' to succeed."

Let me ask you the same question I asked him.

If you were driving down the road and saw a friend pulled over with a flat tire, would you stop to help?

The student acted as if the question were rhetorical. Of course, he would stop. Then I asked if he felt his friend was "using him" or did he just want to help? People love to help others, especially people they trust and respect. Building your network is only building your friendships. Because someone is a part of your network does not mean they will always be in a position to help. Maybe … just maybe … it will be you who helps them someday.

Let's discuss the old adage "It's not what you know, but who you know." Some people believe that no matter how good you are, you're going to have to know somebody to get a job. I'm not one of those people. Allow me to challenge this myth.

Assume for a moment that in 10 years, you will be in a position to hire employees. As luck would have it, your niece is graduating from college. Let's call her Maureen. Maureen is a 4.0 student in electrical engineering at one of the top universities in the world. She is very bright, personable, and capable of filling the position you have advertised.

Your niece submits her résumé to you. Without a doubt, she has one of the top five résumés sitting on your desk. After a series of interviews with all of the most-promising candidates, you have narrowed the pile down to Maureen and one other individual. Do you hire your niece?

⌛ The object of this exercise isn't necessarily to answer "yes" or "no." Did you answer "maybe?" Why?

Let's take another look at the same situation. Ten years from now you are in a position to hire an electrical engineer, and your nephew, Billy, is graduating from college. Your nephew has taken seven years to graduate. While his degree is in electrical engineering, he has changed his major four times. His overall GPA is 2.0. In fact, he had to sit out a semester due to his poor grades.

On your desk are five résumés from people who are top graduates in their classes from some of the country's most prestigious universities. Their skills and abilities far exceed those of your nephew.

⌛ Do you hire your nephew? What did you answer? Now, let's re-examine the old "it's not what you know, but who you know" adage.

We all want to succeed based on our skills and abilities, not because we've benefited from a favor. In 10 years, if you are like most people, you would not hire your own nephew if he were not qualified. The reality is that one must be qualified in order to be considered and get hired. Knowing someone may provide an edge, but it will not get you the job. It is *not* who you know, but *what* you know that ultimately allows you to succeed. What you know will get you the job.

For those of you who are majoring in computer science, networking is not just networking computers; however, the concept makes for a solid analogy: networking is sharing information with others. The difference is that you are the source of this information. The trick is to build a "wide area network" instead of a small "local area network."

Let's begin by preparing a list of the fields that interest you, the people you know employed in those fields, and the companies at which they are employed. Who can you contact for input and advice on your job search?

PLANNING YOUR NETWORK

Field	Contact	Company
_____	_____	_____
_____	_____	_____
_____	_____	_____
_____	_____	_____
_____	_____	_____
_____	_____	_____
_____	_____	_____
_____	_____	_____

Harvey Mackay, a successful businessman and networker extraordinaire, has written a book titled *Dig Your Well Before You're Thirsty: The Only Networking Book You'll Ever Need*. In the book, he offers this insight: "If I had to name the single characteristic shared by all the truly successful people I've met over a lifetime, I'd say it is the ability to create and nurture a network of contacts."

You may not be aware of where jobs are, but someone you know, or someone who knows who you know, will. Creating your list of contacts is the first step in the process. You are only one step away from meeting the right person who knows about the perfect job opportunity.

It may surprise you to discover who your friends may know. On a recent business trip to New York City, I scheduled some time to meet with an old friend, Tamara Tunie. Tammy had been my "first love" when I was four years old. We literally met in a sandbox at the playground. That is why I still get to call her Tammy. Today Tammy serves on Solutions 21's Board of Advisors.

Tammy moved to New York to pursue an acting career and has become quite successful. During my visit we met for lunch. Tammy was a few minutes late because she had been held up filming a scene with her friend, Al Pacino.

I'm amazed that my childhood friend is a friend of Al Pacino. My network is only one step away from "The Godfather." When we were four years old, no one could have predicted the direction our careers and friendships would take. You, too, will also be amazed at who you are "One Step Away" from meeting.

One Step Away List

This list should include a network of people whom you can ask for advice on your job search, to comment on your résumé, to refer you to a prospective employer, and/or to be a reference to that employer.

Roommate's Parents

Name _____   Name _____
Address _____   Address _____
_____   _____
Phone _____   Phone _____
Comments _____   Comments _____
_____   _____

Family Insurance Agents

Name _____   Name _____
Address _____   Address _____
_____   _____
Phone _____   Phone _____
Comments _____   Comments _____
_____   _____

Past Graduates

Name _____   Name _____
Address _____   Address _____
_____   _____
Phone _____   Phone _____
Comments _____   Comments _____
_____   _____

Past Sorority Sisters

Name _____   Name _____
Address _____   Address _____
_____   _____
Phone _____   Phone _____
Comments _____   Comments _____
_____   _____

Past Fraternity Brothers

Name _____   Name _____
Address _____   Address _____
_____   _____
Phone _____   Phone _____
Comments _____   Comments _____
_____   _____

Volunteer Organizations

Name _____   Name _____
Address _____   Address _____
_____   _____
Phone _____   Phone _____
Comments _____   Comments _____
_____   _____

Lawyers

Name _____   Name _____
Address _____   Address _____
_____   _____
Phone _____   Phone _____
Comments _____   Comments _____
_____   _____

Previous Employers

Name _____ Name _____
Address _____ Address _____
_____   _____
Phone _____ Phone _____
Comments _____ Comments _____
_____   _____

Contacts Made Through Previous Employers
(e.g., interned with ABC Company but met people from other businesses)

Name _____ Name _____
Address _____ Address _____
_____   _____
Phone _____ Phone _____
Comments _____ Comments _____
_____   _____

Guest Speakers I've Seen and Met

Name _____ Name _____
Address _____ Address _____
_____   _____
Phone _____ Phone _____
Comments _____ Comments _____
_____   _____

Your list can also include: High School Teachers, Professional Organizations
(e.g., "Society for Human Resource Managers"), Coaches, Family Banker, Local Business People, Doctor, Professors and Dentist)

Name _____ Name _____
Address _____ Address _____
_____   _____
Phone _____ Phone _____
Comments _____ Comments _____
_____   _____

Others

Name _____ Name _____
Address _____ Address _____
_____ _____

Phone _____ Phone _____
Comments _____ Comments _____
_____ _____

Name _____ Name _____
Address _____ Address _____
_____ _____

Phone _____ Phone _____
Comments _____ Comments _____
_____ _____

Name _____ Name _____
Address _____ Address _____
_____ _____

Phone _____ Phone _____
Comments _____ Comments _____
_____ _____

Name _____ Name _____
Address _____ Address _____
_____ _____

Phone _____ Phone _____
Comments _____ Comments _____
_____ _____

Others

Name_____   Name_____
Address_____   Address_____
_____   _____
Phone_____   Phone_____
Comments_____   Comments_____
_____   _____

Name_____   Name_____
Address_____   Address_____
_____   _____
Phone_____   Phone_____
Comments_____   Comments_____
_____   _____

Name_____   Name_____
Address_____   Address_____
_____   _____
Phone_____   Phone_____
Comments_____   Comments_____
_____   _____

Name_____   Name_____
Address_____   Address_____
_____   _____
Phone_____   Phone_____
Comments_____   Comments_____
_____   _____

Implementing Your "One Step Away" List

Once you've developed your "One Step Away" list, you're ready to get to work. But before you can go any further, you must answer the following question: Can I be open-minded?

⌛ Take a moment now to think. Can you be open-minded and accepting of advice from experienced and seasoned professionals?

Have you thought about it? If you cannot be accepting of others' input, there is no need to go any further; however, if you can remain open-minded and use others' input to benefit your job search, then you are ready to move forward.

The first step in this process is to ask for help from everyone on your "One Step Away" list. You are not going to ask these individuals for a job, simply for their input and advice. Your goal is to pass along your "brochure" and expand the number of people who know that you are searching for a job. In a nutshell, you are beginning your advertising campaign.

Your advertising campaign will rely very heavily on three key "network truths." These include:

1. Most people are more comfortable saying "yes" than "no."
2. Most people like to be asked for their input and enjoy giving advice.
3. Most people respect and trust recommendations made by friends.

Understanding these key "network truths" will help you in developing your advertising campaign. You should keep them in mind whether you are using the telephone, sending letters or meeting someone in person.

✏️ The following sample cover letter is designed specifically for your "One Step Away" list. Your goal is to inform, educate, and seek advice.

Sample Cover Letter ("One Step Away" list)

February 21, 20XX

Mr. Walter Bartholomew
123 Carnegie Street
Mifflinwood, USA 11111

Dear Mr. Bartholomew: • Polite opening   • Inform
• Educate

Thank you for taking the time to talk with me on the phone Tuesday evening. I truly appreciate your help and guidance as I conduct my job search.

As you know, I am actively seeking a career opportunity that will be challenging and provide opportunities for growth. My educational background has prepared me with the necessary skills, and my internship at the Community College has given me practical business experience. I am confident that I will be a valuable asset to any firm.

Per our discussion, I am enclosing my résumé. I welcome any input or advice you may be able to offer. I will attempt to call you to follow up on Wednesday at 7:30 p.m. Thank you again. I look forward to speaking with you on Wednesday.

Sincerely,

Rhonda Nelli   • Seek advice

Rhonda Nelli

Enclosure

Your Cover Letter ("One Step Away" list)

_____ Date

_____ Contact's Name
_____ Title
_____ Company
_____ Address
_____ City, State Zip

Dear Mr./Mrs./Ms./Dr.:   • Polite opening   • Inform
                                              • Educate

_____
_____
_____
_____
_____
_____
_____
_____
_____
_____
_____
_____
_____

Sincerely,   • Seek advice

Your Name

Enclosure

Once you have completed the cover letter to your One Step Away list, you will be ready to launch your DIRECT MAIL CAMPAIGN.

This campaign should be a "mail five, phone five" strategy. Every Wednesday you will mail out five résumés and cover letters, and follow up by phone the following Tuesday.

When Tuesday comes, you are now going to actually sit down at the telephone and call your network to seek their advice. At this moment you might be thinking, "I can't call these people and bother them. I don't even really know them!"

Let's examine this thought. In order to do this, you're going to need to take a "think break." Take a few moments now and fast forward 20 years. Your best friend's daughter sends you a copy of her résumé. It is a Tuesday evening at 7 p.m. and you have just finished dinner. The phone rings, and it happens to be this young woman. Are you offended? Do you not want to speak to her? Are you unwilling to offer your input and advice?

⌛ Take a moment to think about this situation. In 20 years, wouldn't you be thrilled to help out your friend's daughter? If you would be thrilled, then the people on your One Step Away list will also enjoy helping you. Review the three basic network truths on page 101.

Are you thinking, "What do I say when I get these people on the telephone?" For starters, try, "Hello, may I please speak to [name]." I know this sounds silly, but think about yourself in 20 years. Would you make it difficult for your friend's daughter to initiate a conversation?

Seeking Advice Over the Telephone

When calling a person from your One Step Away list, you must be prepared for the conversation. Prior to making the call, decide on your questions in advance. Through these questions, you will attempt to do the following:

1. **Seek input on your résumé.** Your goal is to get more input on your résumé, to gain feedback on how effective or ineffective it is. With this question you will be able to determine how well your advertising is being accepted. You may get a great idea on how to make your résumé better. Remember, you are the final decision-maker. You do not need to implement every piece of advice, but you do need to be open to it.

2. **Seek general advice.** You want to seek general advice from your contacts. You may want to ask a question such as, "If you, knowing what you know now, were a college senior, how would you go about searching for a job?"

3. **Ask for references.** Ask your contact if they know of anyone else you can forward your résumé to, using them as a reference. For example you might ask, "Do you know of anyone hiring in my field that I could contact using you as a reference?" You will be surprised at how many good leads are generated this way.

4. **Prepare specific questions beforehand.** Be sure to write down your specific questions in advance. This will ensure that: 1) you are prepared; and 2) you remember to ask the questions. Also, be sure to have a pen and paper handy to record the answers.

- _____
- _____
- _____
- _____
- _____

In order to get the most out of these conversations, be *open-mined*. Consider why is it important to remain open-minded.

⏳ Has anyone ever asked you for advice, and then began to debate your input? Remember when your roommate asked you for help on a research project for the same class you aced the semester before? How did you feel when, after sharing advice based on your first-hand experience, your roommate told you that you were wrong?

He or she may not have said, "You're wrong." The response may have been more subtle. Perhaps he or she said "I'm not sure that would work for me." Or, "That's probably right for you, but I just don't know about this situation." No matter how it was said, the message was clear: **"you're wrong."**

⏳ How did you feel during that conversation? Did you remain open and giving of your thoughts and ideas?

With this in mind, remain open-minded and positive while you are in conversation with your contacts. Avoid phrases such as:

"I'm not very good at..."
"I was going to do that..."
"I'm not sure I could..."
"Yes, but..."
"I'd have a problem with that..."
"I didn't think that would work for me..."

These are professionals you are calling on the telephone. In 20 years, you will be someone's contact. Twenty years from now, you will not be anxious to help a negative, close-minded person. People will give you more input when you are open to receiving it. Do not argue. Remember, they are the experts in these conversations. Avoid negative words such as "can't," "don't," "couldn't," "yes but," "problem," etc.

Now that you have developed your One Step Away list and sought the advice of your contacts, you now must follow up on the references you received. The time has come to begin setting up interviews.

Do you remember in the introduction when we discussed how this book is similar to a self-help book? Everyone wants to improve, but not everyone is willing to accept advice. Without the second round of telephone calls, you are only going half way. It's like putting together your résumé and never mailing it out.

Your second round of telephone calls will be to the references you received from your contacts. With these calls, you will want to:

1. **Call the reference on the telephone and get their address.** Or try to obtain it from your original contact or the new reference's receptionist. Be sure to ask for the full name, including a middle initial, and a title. No matter how common the name, always ask for the correct spelling and recite it back.

2. **Send your reference a résumé with a cover letter.** Your cover letter should mention four things: 1) the name of the person who referred you for the position (or how you learned about the opportunity); 2) your qualifications; 3) your interest in meeting for input on your job search; and 4) a time when you will call to follow up.

3. **Call your reference on the telephone to try to set up a personal appointment.**

✏ Take some time to look at the following sample cover letter. Then create your own. *Note:* This letter will be to someone referred to you by a friend and should be of a business nature. Before you mail the letter, verify that you have spelled the contact's name correctly and make sure that you have included his or her correct title. Punctuation is important (i.e., colon vs. comma in the salutation.) Your placement office can help or consult a book on writing business letters.

Sample Cover Letter (Interview)

March 15, 20XX

Ms. Rita Steiner
Director of Personnel
JS Corporation
647 8th Street, Suite 602
Mifflinwood, USA 11111

- The name of the person who referred you

- Your qualifications for the position

Dear Ms. Steiner:

I am writing in response to the Creative Assistant position that has been brought to my attention by an associate of yours, Walter Bartholomew. My skills and background coincide with your company's current needs, as I understand them.

I am currently a senior at Central Main University. My course of study has been in computers with an emphasis in advertising. Additionally, I have been an active member of the college's advertising club. My internship with ABC Company, a nationally-known advertising/marketing firm, has provided me with the hands-on experience necessary to succeed in the position.

Enclosed please find my résumé for your review. I will follow up with you on March 21 at 8:30 a.m. to see if you need any additional information and to possibly arrange an interview. In the meantime, if you have any questions, I can be reached at 555-2121 after 2 p.m.

Thank you in advance for your time and consideration.

Sincerely,

Rhonda Nelli

Rhonda Nelli

- Your interest in meeting with them
- A time you will call to follow up

Enclosure

Your Cover Letter

_____ Date

_____ Employer's Name
_____ Title
_____ Company
_____ Address
                                          City, State Zip

- The name of the person who referred you
- Your qualifications for the position

Dear Mr./Mrs./Ms./Dr.:

_____
_____
_____
_____
_____
_____
_____
_____
_____
_____
_____
_____

Sincerely,

Your Name

Enclosure

- Your interest in meeting with them
- A time you will call to follow up

Your goal throughout the entire process is to expand your network. Once the people from your One Step Away list have referred you to someone else, begin the process again with this new contact. Try to schedule a face-to-face meeting. If your new contact is not the person who does the interviewing, ask who does. From here, again refer to the third "network truth": *Most people respect and trust the recommendations made by friends.*

Since most people respect and trust their friends' recommendations, you will be more likely to gain a meeting or interview. But once you are "in the door," it will be up to you to generate the necessary interest.

Do not forget that these meetings are interviews. Regardless of where a person chooses to meet with you, treat it as a formal interview. For example, if someone from your One Step Away list asks to meet you for breakfast, understand that it is an interview. Go to the breakfast meeting prepared for an interview. Dress accordingly, have extra résumés, and take along something on which to jot down notes. Be prepared to ask and answer questions.

The same thing applies when you are invited to an "informal" meeting. The person who has invited you is attempting to become familiar with your skills and achieve a certain comfort level with you. *You must help foster this comfort level.* Be prepared. Be ready to ask and answer questions. Your preparation and professionalism will help create the desired comfort level.

⌛ Now let's go back to that first day of college. Do you remember how overwhelming it all seemed? Looking back, were most of your anxieties silly? The same is true with networking/prospecting. You will be surprised at how many opportunities you uncover.

Notes for *Prospecting:*

> *"Look 'em in the eye,
> and tell 'em what you know."*
>
> — Dan Rather,
>   CBS Evening News anchor,
>   quoting his mother's advice

Chapter 6

The Interview

WARNING

If you have flipped open to this chapter to prepare for your first interview but have not read every page prior to this point, stop now and start from the beginning.

The interview process mirrors a sales process. A sales process has seven steps, and each is critical:

1. Product Knowledge
2. Market Knowledge
3. Prospecting
4. Product Presentation
5. Objection Handling
6. Closing the Sale
7. Follow-Up

The previous chapters of this book deal with the first three steps. Without a thorough understanding of each step, you are diminishing your chances for a successful interview. No one single step is more important than the others.

By this point, you now know your product and the market. You've created your brochure, sent out marketing information, addressed the airwaves and worked your network. All of this was to get to the interview.

Once the interview is scheduled, congratulations are in order. The interviewer has looked at your résumé, spent a few moments mulling over your qualifications, and believes you are qualified to work for the company. If you were not qualified, an interviewer would not be wasting his or her valuable time with you.

The interviewer's task is now to determine if there is a match between you and the organization. Does the company have what you want and would you fit into its culture? An article that appeared in *HR Magazine* accurately describes this situation: "Students want meaningful work and a company culture that treats them decently. Employers want college graduates with good interpersonal and communicating skills who can understand bottom-line considerations."[7]

Success at the interview stage hinges on your ability to *present* yourself effectively. Regardless of your chosen career, this will be the key to your success. While there is no magic formula for landing your first job, research shows that communication skills, as demonstrated by written and oral communication during the interview process, are generally viewed as critically important.[8]

Communication skills fall into one of three categories:

1. Non-verbal
2. Interpersonal
3. Problem Solving

Each of these is equally important and cannot be overlooked. Non-verbal communication, especially as demonstrated through poise and neat appearance, is rated highly by human resource professionals as an important factor in a successful initial interview.[9]

Non-Verbal Communication

One of Solutions 21's clients, a nationally-franchised printing company, hired us to help implement a strategic marketing plan. As a part of the plan, the local franchise was expanding its market. This expansion required new personnel, so a hiring campaign was launched.

---

[7] Linda Thornburg, "Employers and Graduates Size Each Other Up," HR Magazine, May 1997.

[8] Charles M. Ray and John J. Stallard - et. al., "Criteria for Business Graduates' Employment: Human Resource Managers' Perceptions.", Vol. 69, Journal of Education for Business, 02-01-1994, pp 140.

[9] Ray, Stallard.

Candidates were sourced from newspapers, local colleges, alumni organizations and through word of mouth. Once a viable candidate was identified, he or she participated in a series of interviews with the local ownership and management. As an additional "filter," I was to conduct the final interview.

All of these final interviews were held at my office. The idea was to see how the candidates presented themselves in a different setting. What I observed through this process should be of value to you as you begin your job search.

Many people let down their guard and showed up for the interview dressed inappropriately. Candidates who were prepared for interviews with the franchise owners felt no need to prepare similarly for a meeting with a consultant. These people were one interview away from a six-figure-income opportunity, and they did not maintain their focus.

The first mistake was to assume these sessions were less important than the others. *Never* assume any interaction with a prospective employer or network contact is unimportant. *Always* be prepared.

The first form of communication humans learn is non-verbal communication. As infants, before our speech skills develop, we learn to communicate without words. Even as we develop other forms of communication, we continue to communicate non-verbally, sending and receiving "cues," both consciously and unconsciously, that either reinforce or undermine what we are saying.

Professional speakers, politicians, lawyers and others whose success rests on their public speaking abilities, understand this key fact: very little of what we actually say is critical to effective communication. In fact, only seven percent of the spoken word accounts for what is communicated between two people. *How* we say something, our tone of voice, makes up 38 percent, while a whopping 55 percent of all communication is derived from non-verbal cues.[10]

What you say is important, but how you say it and how you look saying it is far more crucial. Non-verbal communication is a science all its own, and as you prepare for your job search, you need not become an expert. There are three areas, however, in which you should develop some expertise: professional dress, the handshake and tone of voice.

---

[10] David Lewis, The Secret Language of Success: Using Body Language to Get What You Want, Carrol and Graf, 1988.

Professional Dress

How you look represents a major portion of any message you will communicate. The manner in which you dress, by itself, speaks volumes.

One of your major priorities as a recent or soon-to-be graduate should be to upgrade your wardrobe. This is an important step. With all of the money you have invested in your education, do not undermine your chances now. A few hundred dollars could be the difference between success and failure. (See page 119.)

When putting together the right wardrobe, you need to focus on all of the components that make up a professional outfit: the suit, shirt/blouse, tie/scarf, shoes, belt, and socks/hose. Do not overlook any of these, as they all work together to make a very important statement about you as a professional. But don't worry, achieving the right appearance won't set you back thousands of dollars. If properly coordinated, your interviewing outfit should cost less than $400, while allowing you to present yourself very professionally.

An interviewer will make certain allowances for recently-graduated college students. You do not need a $2,000 wardrobe for your interviews. But you do need to present yourself in a well-groomed, professional manner. Your goal for an interview is to be so perfectly groomed that what you are wearing is not noticeable.

In other words, your professional appearance should be a neutral point. It will not increase your chances of landing the job; however, the way you are dressed and groomed can detract from your interview and lessen your chances to secure the position.

Since 55 percent of our communication is non-verbal, professional appearance is critical. After you have assembled a professional wardrobe, give it a test run. Conduct a dress rehearsal.

Have a friend take several photographs of you "in uniform" from several different angles. A private photo shoot might feel uncomfortable at first, but try to have some fun with it. What you will learn could be the difference between "just a job" and your perfect job.

Ask your friend to take photos from all angles: front, right, left and back. Be sure the pictures include shots of you in both sitting and standing positions. This is how an interviewer will see you.

When you have the developed photos in hand, examine each one closely. Are you comfortable with how you look, or should you make adjustments? Look at your networking list. Whose opinion do you respect enough to send copies of the photos? Send out all angles and ask for feedback.

Do not try to short-cut this step by merely looking in the mirror. The mirror will lie, a photograph will not. A mirror image is a reverse image, which means it is, in a way, incorrect. A photo will show you exactly how you look to others, not how you look to yourself.

These exercises are important for two major reasons. First, working on your professional appearance prior to interviewing will allow you to assess your look and make any necessary corrections. Second, it will ensure that you are *completely confident* about your appearance when heading into an interview.

Not only will you have seen yourself as others will see you, but you will also have had the opportunity to draw on feedback from people you respect and make adjustments prior to the day of the interview. Once you have taken these steps, you will have eliminated one of your key worries. Now you can better concentrate on the interview itself, feeling confident that you've addressed 55 percent of your communication.

Men's Wardrobe

Do's	Don'ts
• Navy blue or gray conservative suit	• No sports coats
• White, cotton blend, well-tailored, ironed shirt	• No silk shirts
• Fashionable, but not bold, tie	• No makeup
• Dark-color, over-the-calf socks	• No bow ties
• Dark-color shoes to match belt	• No rubber-soled shoes
• Leather shoes with leather soles	• No Italian-cut shoes
• Avoid trendy hair cuts	• No belt *and* suspenders
• Facial hair should be properly groomed (or better yet, shave it)	• No skin showing over socks
• Nails should be clean and trimmed	• No earrings
	• No cologne
	• No items identifying personal beliefs

Women's Wardrobe

Do's	Don'ts
• Blouse should contrast with suit	• No dresses
• Natural-color hose	• No open weaves
• 1"- 2" heels	• No skin showing
• Modest hairstyle	• No dark hose
• If hair is dyed, be sure to dye roots	• No bright-colored shoes
• Subdued, natural makeup	• No flats or spike heels
• Small earrings	• No items identifying personal beliefs
• Nails should be clean and trimmed, natural polish	• No attention-grabbing jewelry
	• No perfume

Shopping List

Men

Conservative Business Suit		$200
2 Dress Shirts	($25 each)	$50
2 Pairs of Dress Socks	($5 each)	$10
2 Ties	($15 each)	$30
Dress Shoes		$60
Leather Belt (to match shoes)		$20
	Total	$370

Women

Skirted Business Suit		$200
2 Blouses	($30 each)	$60
2 Pairs of Hose	($5 each)	$10
Dress Shoes		$50
	Total	$320

For those items where it is suggested that you purchase two, it is always a good idea to have a backup in case you have two interviews in one week!

The Handshake

The handshake is a ritual as old as time. It can tell a great deal about a person. David Lewis, in his book, *The Secret Language of Success: Using Body Language to Get What You Want*, writes, "The language of the handshake is as subtle and complex as the ritual of ancient Chinese courts."[11]

An initial meeting offers you the chance, through a handshake, to make a solid first impression. The handshake will be one of your first opportunities to set the tone for the interview. Remember, consciously or unconsciously, the other person is making judgments about you and how you present yourself.

A handshake is a deceptively simple act, which can be evaluated through six key factors:

1. Appearance: Hand and nails clean, fingernails properly groomed.
2. Texture: Rough or soft.
3. Dryness: Sweaty palms or dry.
4. Pressure used: "Dead fish," "bone breaker," "just right."
5. Time in contact: How long hands are grasped.
6. Style: One-handed or two-handed grasp.[12]

It is my personal opinion that you can't go wrong with a handshake by heeding these four points of advice:

1. Keep your hands dry.
2. Make sure your hands are clean and well-groomed.
3. Use moderate pressure.
4. Hold the handshake for approximately three to five seconds.

---

[11] Lewis

[12] Lewis

Arrive early for your interview so you can spend a few moments in the restroom. Take this time to adjust your appearance, fix your hair and wash your hands. Hold your hands under the warm water for a few moments. When you are nervous, your hands tend to become cold and sweaty. Washing them with warm water will help.

Tone of Voice

Since 38 percent of effective communication derives from your tone of voice, how you say something becomes very important during the interview process. A few tricks and a little preparation on your part will go a long way toward helping you present yourself in the best light.

While the way you speak is important, do not be overly concerned that your voice will sound nervous. To some degree everyone is nervous during an interview. An interviewer will understand this; however, the better you can control the tone and pace of your voice, the better impression you will make.

When a person is nervous, he or she will tend to speak too quickly. Make a conscious effort to *slow down* while speaking. Try to concentrate on speaking slower, especially at the beginning of the interview. As the session progresses, you will become more relaxed and your speech will assume a more natural pace.

While you are in the restroom making those few last-minute adjustments, take some time to *calm down*. Professional speakers have learned a trick to help them relax before giving a speech: breathing. Before any presentation, I always take some time for myself prior to going on stage. During these quiet moments I take deep breaths, inhaling on a five count and exhaling on a five count. It's amazing how well this works.

The other thing I do is visualize a successful speech. I want to see what my talk will look like. While I am taking my deep breaths, I visualize a positive outcome.

Prior to your interview, take a few moments to breathe and visualize your success. See the interviewer becoming enthusiastic over your responses. Hear him or her ask you back for another interview. Better yet, picture this person offering you the job. Develop a positive mental picture, and your chances for success will skyrocket.

General Points for Interviewing

- Never assume any interaction is unimportant. Always be prepared.

- Do not undermine your chances for success with an unprofessional wardrobe.

- Have yourself photographed in your wardrobe and ask for feedback.

- Use a proper handshake to make a favorable first impression.

- At the beginning of an interview, consciously try to talk slowly. Nervousness will cause you to speak too quickly.

- Breathe, breathe, breathe, and relax.

- Visualize your success.

Interpersonal Communication

Human resources professionals rank ability to communicate as *the* most important consideration when choosing whom to hire. Oral communication, listening and interpersonal communication were cited as very important or important by 90 percent of respondents to a national survey of HRM professionals.[13]

If you are looking to enter a technical field, do not believe communication does not apply to you. Regardless of the field, technical or non-technical, effective communication is key. *Computerworld Magazine* warns recent graduates, "If you want a career in [information technology] today, you need much more than expertise in SQL, PowerBuilder and client/server. Without the so-called "soft" skills — chief among them, written and oral communication skills, and the ability to get along with others — you can probably kiss your chances of a successful IT career good-bye."[14]

One way to demonstrate your ability to communicate during an interview is to listen effectively, respond naturally, and ask questions.

---

[13] Charles M. Ray and John J. Stallard - et. al., "Criteria for Business Graduates' Employment: Human Resource Managers' Perceptions.", Vol. 69, Journal of Education for Business, 02-01-1994, pp 140.

[14] Alice LaPlante, "Lighten Up!", Computerworld, April 1997.

An interview serves many purposes. For a moment, put yourself in the shoes of the employer. Employers, during interviews, seek to discover whether or not the individual is a good match for both the available position and the company. That doesn't necessarily mean anything good or bad about the interviewee. What it does means is that the interviewer is looking for someone with the right combination of skills, talents, educational background, and experience to fit into the organization and further its goals.

The good news is, you will be the only person involved in the interviewing process who "knows the product." This being the case, you should be as relaxed as possible and in a good mindset to group all your responses in an order that shows focus and direction. Now is the time to use your funnels.

Have you, or any of your friends, ever had an interview that simply bombed? When you were sitting around discussing this failed interview, did you discuss the interviewer's skills? For example, did you, or your friend assess the interview using phrases such as these:

- "He didn't ask me any questions."
- "She seemed to bounce around throughout the entire interview."
- "I knew more about her company than she did."
- "I don't think he had ever interviewed before."

The truth of the matter is that the interviewer may not have interviewed before. As we discussed previously, not all interviewers will be proficient at interviewing. That is why you need to be proficient with your funnels.

In many interviews you will be asked multi-part questions. For example: "Why did you choose Central Main University, and how did you choose computer science as your major?" The purpose of this question is to see if you can thoughtfully respond to both points. This will allow the interviewer to measure your analytical and creative thought processes. It will also allow you to demonstrate your listening skills.

Many times a person will respond to only one part of the question. Nervousness, lack of focus and a failure to prepare can leave the interviewee vulnerable to multi-part questions. This can be especially true when the questions seem unrelated, as in "Tell me about your work with the History Club and about your last summer job."

The interviewer may be asking these seemingly unrelated questions because she is not a good interviewer, or because she is, and wants to gauge your thought process. Either way, it will not matter if you are prepared and have studied your funnels. You should be able to tackle multi-part questions with ease. When the question is asked, you will instantly identify which of your funnels to use for the answer. You will be able to answer confidently and demonstrate solid listening skills.

One of the most common mistakes made during an interview is also one of the most damaging: failing to *ask* questions. When going in for an interview, many individuals mistakenly assume that their sole purpose is to answer questions. This is not true. *The purpose of the interview is to determine a match.*

For your role in this process, you will need to ask questions. Asking questions initiates dialogue and allows for a more relaxed and interactive session. Your ability to converse with the interviewer will allow you to demonstrate your interpersonal/communication skills. The interviewer wants to see that you need more information and are capable of interacting with others. If you do not ask questions, the interviewer may arrive at one of six conclusions about you:

1. You are a "know-it-all."
2. You are not seriously interested in the position or the company.
3. You are not bright enough to formulate your own questions.
4. You are desperate and will take any job.
5. You don't care about the direction of your career.
6. You are not good at one-on-one interaction.

Any of these conclusions will be a negative and can exclude you from further consideration. The interviewer wants to be confident that you are right for them and that they are right for you. Asking questions will help instill this confidence. Just as the interviewer will ask a question based on your previous response, you should ask questions based on his or her last response. This is particularly important during your second, third, and even fourth interview. Allow me to use myself as an example.

During my senior year in college, I had an interview with IBM. The corporation's local office sent in a marketing vice president to do the initial interviewing. The first session was scheduled to last 40 minutes and was designed to serve as a quick "weeding out" process.

The Interview

Much to my surprise, this vice president and I hit it off. My 40-minute interview lasted an hour and a half. I was handling his questions, asking my questions, and really rolling along. Afterwards, I felt good about my chances.

The local vice president passed me on for another interview at the district office. Once there, I encountered another person who had a distinctly different personality than the vice president. For some reason, and I know the reason now, this interview did not go well. When it came time for me to ask questions, I responded with, "Oh, Mr. So and So and I talked extensively and he answered all of my questions." A few seconds later, the interview ended. Within a week, I received a rejection letter. I could not figure out how I had failed.

I later realized that I did not assume responsibility for the process. I was unprepared to ask questions. The second interview was not going well, and I wanted out of there as quickly as possible. I didn't ask questions; therefore, I came across as unable to interact effectively.

If you take nothing else from this book, take this one piece of advice: *ask questions*. In your first interview, did you ask a question that caused the interviewer to get excited? Did she put down her pencil and move aside her notebook in order to enthusiastically respond to your question? Was his response animated and did he show excitement while answering your question? Did he compliment you on such an insightful query? If so, there is one thing you know for certain — *it was a great question*. If you know that you already have asked a great question in your first interview, *ask it again* in subsequent interviews.

Once you have determined that you have asked a dynamite question, keep it in your repertoire and get as much mileage out of it as you can. By asking the same questions of multiple interviewers within the same organization, you can compare the responses and gain further insight into the company. For example, a vice president and a human resources director may have completely different ideas on the company's long-term strategy. By comparing these answers, you will have even more information at your disposal.

When I first began interviewing for jobs, I truly believed that everything discussed was somehow recorded. Anything and everything was handed off to the next interviewer and gone through with a fine-tooth comb. I was certain that if I asked the same question twice it would exclude me from further consideration. In reality, no one knew the questions I had asked previously. Everything was not recorded in great detail. I could have asked the same question twice. If I had a good question, I should have felt comfortable using it again and again.

The interviewing process is a lot like a professional golf tournament. A golf tournament consists of four rounds with the champion being determined by the cumulative score at the end of the fourth round. Quite frequently, the interview process consists of at least four rounds — sometimes more. As I look back on my interview with IBM, I realize now that I was leading the tournament after the first round, but after the first nine holes of the second round, I had slipped badly. The interviewer gave me an opportunity to make a comeback when she asked if I had any questions.

In truth, I could not summon up the courage to continue. I refused to take control of my situation and play the final nine holes. Instead, I chose to disqualify myself. I should have asked questions.

There are two basic types of questions: open-ended and closed-ended. Open-ended questions require long, descriptive answers. They are great for generating discussion. Closed-ended questions are those that can be answered in one or two words. Here are some examples of each:

Open-Ended Questions

- "Where do you see XYZ Corporation in 10 years?"
- "Please explain the type of career paths I can choose at XYZ Corporation."
- "Tell me about the strategic partnerships you have formed with other organizations."
- "Tell me about the history of this product line."

Closed-Ended Questions

- "Will XYZ Corporation add products over the next 10 years?"
- "Is there a career path for new hires?"
- "Have you formed strategic partnerships with other organizations?"
- "How long have you offered this product line?"

The best questions to ask are open-ended questions. These questions are much more conversational in nature and will help to facilitate discussion. Open-ended questions also tend to require more conceptual responses, which serve to highlight your analytical and creative thought processes.

Closed-ended questions should only be used to elicit short, definitive answers. Often you think you have asked an open-ended question, but receive a closed response. For example, "Have you formed any strategic partnerships with other organizations?" The interviewer may respond with a yes or no answer. Don't panic. Simply reply, "Tell me about it."

When asking questions, concentrate on gathering information about the position, the company, its products and the marketplace. Do not ask questions that might make you appear selfish or unmotivated. Early in the interviewing process, avoid questions about salary, vacation, holiday time, raises and length of work day. These questions will make you look shallow and uncommitted.

Let's again fast forward 20 years to when you are conducting an interview. You are looking for an entry-level, college-educated customer service representative. The position can eventually lead to other opportunities within your firm. A customer service representative needs to be detail-oriented, possess good writing skills, and be able to deal with people. Furthermore, this position requires a committed individual who will work diligently to solve any customer problems, even if it requires extra effort.

The candidate you are interviewing seems to possess all of the necessary credentials. Her résumé shows that all of the relevant courses have been completed. She also has participated in several extracurricular activities that seemingly demonstrate an ability to work with people.

After you have asked several questions, you begin to describe the opportunities for advancement. You then turn to this bright, young, qualified candidate and ask if she has any questions. She responds with, "Yes, I do. What time do you start in the morning and what time does the work day end?"

What would you think? Is this person committed? Is she dedicated? Will she handle a customer complaint from start to finish? Can she get up in the morning?

The candidate might have meant something totally different, but the phraseology of the question will leave only negative thoughts in the interviewer's mind. The candidate might have been thinking, "I really like to get up early and work late. Will the office be open before and after hours?"

You would have never known the intent of the question because of the way it was asked. If the candidate had asked an open-ended question about the advancement opportunities you would not have had any negative thoughts. Save your closed-ended questions until the end of the interviewing process. In the final stages, you can discuss things like vacation, benefits, salary, raises, length of work day and advancement opportunities.

When you are in an interview and are tempted to say, "No, I don't have any questions. You have answered them all," remember my interview at IBM. Ask questions and always realize that you are in a tournament that figuratively lasts four rounds. You need to perform well in each round.

Take a moment to review your list of strengths and weaknesses. Your number one strength is courage. This is the single greatest attribute you will need in order to take control when the "golf tournament" begins to go badly. Summon your courage, take control, and implement the techniques you have learned throughout this book.

✏️ For the following exercise, list questions that you would/could ask your prospective employer. In preparing this list, you may want to ask your placement office for their input.

Asking Questions

- "What are the goals of XYZ Corporation?"
- "Tell me about your growth plans."
- "Where do you see the company in five years?"
- "What types of ongoing skill development programs do you offer?"
- "Could you tell me about your own professional growth at XYZ Corporation?"
- "What types of technology are used within this organization?"
- "How will my job performance be evaluated?"

?_____
?_____
?_____
?_____
?_____
?_____
?_____
?_____
?_____
?_____

If all of your prepared questions have been answered during the session, ask the interviewer to expand on his or her answers. For example, "Could you tell me more about your growth plans?"

Problem Solving

Producing Results

In assessing your fit with the organization, the interviewer will be looking to gauge how well you might produce for the company. If hired, you will be expected to become a productive, contributing employee. One way the interviewer will determine your ability is to examine your problem-solving skills.

At Microsoft, for example, interviewees are commonly asked such questions as how they would weigh an airplane without a scale, or how much water flows through the Mississippi River each day.[15]

The point is not to arrive at the "right" answer, but to determine a thought process. The interviewer is more interested in what information is requested, what questions are asked and the nature of an applicant's problem solving skills.[16]

Human resource experts believe that past performance will predict future behavior.[17] Potential new hires are expected to demonstrate that they can be expected to perform at a high level. David Pritchard, director of recruiting for Microsoft, says, "One of the things we look for is smarts and experience, but we also want to know what they will bring here over the long term. Are they flexible? Can they learn new concepts?"[18] In short, can they produce results?

Since interviewing is analogous to sales, let's reexamine the sales process. Sales professionals understand that they must prove the worth of their products or services. The successful sales professional knows that a buyer is only concerned with results. If you are going to be successful in selling yourself, you must first understand:

1. How and why people buy.
2. How the best sales professionals position their products.

Take a moment to think about some of your recent purchases. For example, why did you buy your last stick or can of deodorant? Was it because of the label, package

---

[15] Ron Lieber; David Pritchard Research Associate Erin M. Davies, "Managing: Ideas & Solutions/From the Front/Wired for Hiring: Microsoft's Slick Recruiting Machine", Fortune, Feb. 1996.
[16] Lieber and Pritchard.
[17] Thornburg.
[18] Lieber and Pritchard.

or price? All of these things may have contributed to your decision, but didn't you buy it because of the result you would achieve? If the package was nice, the label was appealing and the price was right, but it would not deodorize you, would you have purchased the product?

The bottom line is, consciously or unconsciously, people buy because of the result they will receive from a product. Therefore, you need to learn how to position yourself in terms of the results that can be derived from hiring you. An interviewer cares about what you will achieve for the organization; what problems you will solve.

The most successful sales professionals learn how to position their products or services with results in mind. Less-than-successful sales people only talk about a product's components. A component is simply a part of the whole. Talking about a product's components, without detailing how each component contributes to the whole, and ultimately to the results to be expected from the product, is only telling part of the story.

While you were constructing your funnels, you were also detailing your product's individual components. Each item on your résumé is simply a single component of your product. Your task is to show how each one translates into the desired result an employer is seeking. To do this, you will need to study your CAR.

C = **C**omponent
A = **A**dvantage
R = **R**esult

Each component of your résumé needs to relate directly to an advantage. The advantage will highlight why the component is important, and why it is a necessary and useful part of the whole. In turn, this advantage translates into a desired result.

Let's look at an example of how this works:

Component:	• Member of Student Government
Advantage:	• Highly competitive
	• Balanced duties with academic workload
	• Learned and practiced team work
Result:	• Can maintain focus on more than one area at a time
	• Can manage a work schedule to accommodate various projects
	• Can function well within a group atmosphere

In order to become proficient with the CAR method, you will need to study and memorize a few key transitional phrases. These phrases, once they are committed to memory and you are comfortable in using them, will provide you with the confidence to move smoothly through each component of your résumé to emphasize the result.

Transitional Phases

Since I have:	Component
I have learned to:	Advantage
Proving, demonstrating or illustrating that:	Result

Examples:

Since I have:	participated in Student Government.
I have learned to:	balance more than one critical assignment at a time.
Proving that:	I am capable of successfully managing several projects simultaneously.

Since I have:	participated in Student Government.
I have learned to:	understand my role within a team or group.
Demonstrating that:	I can perform successfully both independently and within the framework of a team.

Since I have:	participated in Student Government.
I have learned to:	discipline myself to achieve goals.
Illustrating that:	I am self-motivated and goal-oriented.

By learning and practicing these transitional phrases, you will be able to make your interview much more interesting. Highlighting the results you can offer an employer will increase your chances for success.

In determining your own components, look at the following list and ask yourself if you have any of these skills. You may also want to refer to pages 8, 16-17 and 18.

Skills Employers Are Seeking

Communication Skills
- Do you have good writing skills?
- Do you demonstrate good listening skills?
- Do you possess excellent speaking skills?

Problem-Solving Skills
- Are you creative?
- Are you adaptable?
- Are you detail-oriented?
- Do you follow up?
- Do you use your time efficiently?

Leadership Skills
- Are you persuasive?
- Are you energetic?
- Do you have a positive attitude?
- Do you lead by example?

Motivational Skills
- Are you goal-oriented?
- Are you a self-starter?
- Do you possess a strong self image?
- Do you have a strong work ethic?

Teamwork
- Are you able to motivate others?
- Are you a peacemaker?
- Do you work well within a group?
- Do you have good interpersonal skills?

As the interview progresses and the conversation zeros in on your many "product components," your goal should be to highlight the "product results." If you have practiced the transitional phrases, you will be able to highlight the appropriate results that hiring you will produce for the company.

Your CAR will be helpful when the interviewer focuses on a single component of your résumé. For example, "What have you learned from your experience with Student Government?" At this point you can respond smoothly and confidently.

Your response, which you ideally have practiced several times, would be something like, "Since I have participated in Student Government, I have learned to balance more than one critical assignment at a time, proving that I am capable of successfully managing several projects at once."

For the following exercise, refer to "Skills Employers Are Seeking," on the preceding page, and also pages 8, 16-17 and 18. For each component and advantage, list three to five results using the words "proving," "demonstrating," or "illustrating." Practice until the process becomes natural.

Since I have (Component):
_____

I have learned to (Advantage):
_____

Proving, demonstrating or illustrating that (Result):
_____
_____
_____
_____
_____
_____

Since I have (Component):

I have learned to (Advantage):

Proving, demonstrating or illustrating that (Result):

Since I have (Component):

I have learned to (Advantage):

Proving, demonstrating or illustrating that (Result):

Since I have (Component):

I have learned to (Advantage):

Proving, demonstrating or illustrating that (Result):

Since I have (Component):

I have learned to (Advantage):

Proving, demonstrating or illustrating that (Result):

Since I have (Component):

I have learned to (Advantage):

Proving, demonstrating or illustrating that (Result):

Since I have (Component):

I have learned to (Advantage):

Proving, demonstrating or illustrating that (Result):

Since I have (Component):
_____

I have learned to (Advantage):
_____

Proving, demonstrating or illustrating that (Result):
_____
_____
_____
_____

Since I have (Component):
_____

I have learned to (Advantage):
_____

Proving, demonstrating or illustrating that (Result):
_____
_____
_____
_____

Since I have (Component):
_____

I have learned to (Advantage):
_____

Proving, demonstrating or illustrating that (Result):
_____
_____
_____
_____

Notes for *The Interview:*

Notes for *The Interview:*

> *"You win battles...by knowing the enemy's timing, and thus using a timing which the enemy does not expect."*
>
> — Miyamoto Musashi,
>   17th century samurai and Japan's greatest swordsman

Chapter 7

Closing The Sale

If you asked the world's top sales professionals why they are so successful, they would likely find their success hard to explain. But if you observed them in action, you would discover that they have committed themselves to many of the principles outlined in this book. You would also discover another very important characteristic about these successful people: *they work through their fears.* The top salespeople and the average salespeople experience the same fears and anxieties, but the top performers do not allow these feelings to stop them.

Have you ever wanted to ask someone out on a date? How did you feel as you were summoning the courage to ask the question? If you felt nervous and anxious, why? Was it the fear of rejection? Take a moment to think about that feeling.

Contrary to popular belief, inability to deal with rejection is not the reason salespeople fail. It is their *inability to open themselves up to rejection* that causes them to fail. No one likes rejection. Successful salespeople, on the other hand, take each "no" as a step closer to a "yes."

There have been several studies done on the sales profession. Study after study confirms the fact that it takes at least seven "no's" to get to one "yes." In other words, a person must overcome seven negative obstacles, either an outright "no" or a strong objection, in order to achieve a successful close.

What separates the truly great salespeople from the pack is their recognition of this fact. Since they realize the need for seven "no's," they try to get them out of the way as quickly as possible. They want to be in control of the situation. By seeking these "no's," they are capable of answering the objections and overcome any obstacle.

People are afraid to seek the negative response. Most would prefer to allow a person to think it over than to probe for objections. Usually, given enough time to think it over, a person will experience some buyer's remorse and say no. Unfortunately, at that point the salesperson isn't around to address the objection.

What all of this means to you is that you need to understand the reality of a rejection letter. You are always going to open yourself up to rejection by entering into the interviewing process. Your challenge is to identify and deal with obstacles while you are still face-to-face with the interviewer. The easy way out is to not ask the difficult questions and, ultimately, receive the rejection letter.

Your challenge is to draw on your number one strength: courage. Ask the difficult questions. Only by doing this, are you able to address an objection and get another opportunity to close the sale.

When talking about closing the sale, I am not just speaking about asking for the job in the final interview. You need to prepare yourself to ask for what you want during each phase of the interview process. If you are on the telephone and want to set up an interview, ask for it. If you are meeting a person from your network, ask for referrals. If you are in the initial stages, ask, "What is the next step?" and, "Will you be recommending me for that step?" Finally, as you get toward the end, ask for the job.

For every one employer who would be put off by your asking for the job, there are a thousand who will be impressed. Asking for what you want is a sign of courage, determination, confidence and professionalism. Remember, you hope to be working for this person/company. Once you are an employee, they will want you to champion their cause. Therefore, they will respect your efforts to champion your own cause.

Closing the sale will be slightly different during each step of the process. If you are meeting a person from your network for lunch, and you are seeking referrals, you may want to ask, "Now that you've had an opportunity to review my résumé and speak with me, are there any concerns you might have in referring me to someone you know?"

Once you have asked the question, you need to be prepared for an honest answer. If he or she does not have any concerns, then you can proceed with your next question. You might simply say, "Is there anyone you can think of who I can contact using your name to attain an interview?" Do not assume you will automatically receive a reference, but don't let this possibility stop you from asking. If, on the other hand, the person does voice concerns, you need to be able to address them.

During the interview process, closing the sale means securing a move to the next step. In the beginning stages, ask what exactly the next step is. When you are presented with an opportunity to ask questions, one of your last should always be, "What is the next step?" When you know the answer to this question, you will be able to plan your close. (Add this question to your list on page 129.)

Often an interviewee fails to close because he or she is given a huge dose of encouragement. An interviewer may say something like, "George, we are considering several other candidates. Obviously, you would not have progressed this far if we didn't think your qualifications were sound. I will be getting back to you."

At that point, George is probably feeling pretty good. Why would he want to push it? Why would he want to place any undo pressure on the interviewer and ask her more specific questions? After all, she said she would be getting back to him.

Couldn't the statement, "I will be getting back to you" also mean, "Watch your mail for a rejection letter?" A letter is getting back to you. Let's take a moment and analyze the entire statement.

Statement	What it could really mean to you
• *"George, we are considering several other candidates."*	• *"George, we are considering several other candidates and, if any one of them accepts the job, we will not be offering it to you."*
• *"Obviously, you would not have progressed this far if we didn't think your qualifications were sound."*	• *"Your qualifications are pretty good, but there are 10 or 12 other candidates we like better."*
• *"I will be getting back to you."*	• *"I really don't want to have to tell you "no" now, so I'll take the easy way out. You should watch your mail."*

No matter how good you feel when an interviewer says "I will get back to you," you still do not have the job. Let's not confuse feeling good with getting a paycheck. You need to ask for the job. You could say something like, "You know, Ms. Smith, I really appreciate that you are considering my qualifications, and I truly understand that I am one of the final candidates. Could you share with me a reason why you wouldn't offer me the job today?"

What you have done here is try to flush out a "no." Now, the interviewer will need to give you an objection or offer you the job. Once you have heard the objection, you can then attempt to answer it. By drawing out the objection, you are able to gain control of the situation and create an opportunity to close the sale.

Remember, it takes an average of seven "no's" to get to the final "yes." The first step in getting to that final "yes" is to summon the courage to open yourself up to rejection. The next step is to begin eliminating the "no's" by answering the interviewer's objections and concerns.

The Dream Retirement Method (DRM)

Handling objections is a learned skill. No one is born with the inherent ability to correctly address concerns. Top salespeople commit themselves to learning this skill. By learning how to handle objections, they are better able to work through their fear of rejection.

Ultimately, closing the sale means getting the job. Getting the job means you are one step closer to retiring. Retiring means moving to your dream home on the beach or in the mountains, or spending all day on the golf course or doing whatever it is you choose to do.

Closing the sale and landing your first job is the first step toward building your dream retirement. In other words, your first job is the foundation of your career. All good dream retirement homes need to be built on a solid foundation.

⌛ Take a moment to visualize your dream home being built. You have found the perfect spot. The design work is done. All of the plans have been finalized. The time to start building has arrived. The construction crew shows up with the backhoes and bulldozers. The excavation process begins. What do you see?

The back hoes and bulldozers start digging a hole for the foundation. Once the foreman thinks it's deep enough, he will check to see if he is finished. If he is, he will begin to pour the foundation. If not, he will:

- **Dig deeper**
- **Remeasure**

Once the hole is deep enough, the crew will then:

- **Target the concrete**
- **Pour the concrete**
- **Finish the concrete**

The same process applies to handling objections.

Step 1: Dig deeper. The interview is winding down. You have answered all of the interviewer's questions and asked all of your questions. Just like the foreman measuring the hole, you will now check to see if you're ready to move forward by *asking a closing question*. For example: "Will you be recommending me for the next step?" If the interviewer says yes, you have dug deep enough. Clarify your understanding of the next step and thank him or her for the support. The interviewer may say something other than yes, for example:

- *"We have several other candidates, and I'm not sure."*
- *"We'll be in touch."*
- *"Your qualifications look good, but I will have to let you know."*
- *"No, I don't think so."*

If so, now is the time to dig deeper. At this point, you will want to ask a question such as, "You seem to have some concern/hesitation about recommending me. Do you mind if I ask what it is?"

Listen carefully to the answer. If, for example, the interviewer says, "Well, I was hoping to hire someone with better computer skills." Do not assume you understand what "better computer skills" means. Now is not the time to answer. Dig deeper. You need to fully understand the objection. Ask a more probing question: "Do you mind if I ask exactly what kind of computer skills you are looking for?"

The interviewer then must narrow the broad objection. The response might be, "I'm looking for someone who is both PC and Macintosh literate." Even though you have experience with both the PC and Macintosh platforms, this is still not the time to answer. Now, you will need to re-measure.

Step 2: Remeasure. You have found more ground to cover so you must remeasure. Remeasuring means *restating your understanding of the objection*. This will help to clarify the objection for both you and the interviewer.

Your response might be, "So, the ideal candidate will have a knowledge of both the PC and Macintosh?" You have now remeasured and clarified your understanding of the objection. The interviewer may either further clarify the objection or simply say, "Yes, that's right."

Step 3: Target. Any good construction worker knows that when pouring cement, a form is necessary for the pour to be *exactly on target*. This minimizes waste, maximizes strength and ensures proper coverage. The same thing applies when you are answering an objection; you must target the response so that you accurately, effectively and completely address the concern.

Targeting your response means isolating the objection so that you remove the last hurdle to a successful close. Your next statement could be, "If I am hearing you correctly, my background would be a good fit with XYZ Corporation if I were both PC and Macintosh literate? Is that correct?"

Once you've attained a "yes" to this question, you can proceed to Step 4; however, if the answer is "no," there are other concerns that you need to understand and confront. (Repeat Steps 1 through 3.)

Step 4: Pour. Since you have targeted the objection, you can now "pour the concrete" by *answering the objection*. If you have dug deep enough, properly remeasured and targeted your response effectively, the answer should satisfy the objection. "While all of my course work has been done on a PC, I have significant experience with the Macintosh platform. In fact, as chairman of the History Club, I do all of our work on a Mac."

Most of the time, you will be able to fully answer the objection. But if you are unable to do so, you will need to highlight other results you can deliver. This is another critical reason to study and know how to drive your CAR. For example, "While all of my course work is done on a PC, I am a quick study and will pick up the Mac before I start with XYZ Corporation. Since I have a double major, I have learned to balance several priorities, *demonstrating that* I am capable of learning the Mac while completing my course work."

Remember, problem solving is very important. If you have encountered an objection you cannot overcome by relating past experience, draw on your problem-solving abilities. You certainly have solved other problems in the past, now is the time to demonstrate that you can also solve this one. Use your past experience in overcoming this new hurdle. What situations similar to this have you encountered?

Step 5: Finish. After you have satisfactorily answered the objection, you can now complete the process. Just as the construction foreman would never pour the concrete and then walk away, you can't leave your foundation unfinished. You must now confirm the interviewer's understanding of your answer.

Finishing, or confirming, means simply asking the interviewer, "Does that answer your concern?" If the answer is "yes," you are finished and can ask for the job again. If the answer is "no," or "not quite," you should repeat Steps 1 through 4 before asking yet again.

Don't lose sight of how many negative responses it takes to close a sale. On average, you may have to repeat this process seven times in order to receive the job offer. The process is the same, whether you are asking to be recommended for the next step or asking for the job itself. You must flush out objections, make sure you understand each one and effectively address them. Your ability to utilize this process to its fullest, will set you apart from your competition.

Example of Dream Retirement Method (DRM)

Closing the sale

Interviewer: "We'll be in touch."

Incorrect response:	**Correct response:**
"Thank you."	"Thank you for your time. Can I ask you one last question? Will you be recommending me for the next step?"

Dig deeper

Interviewer: "Possibly, we have several other candidates, and I'm not sure right now."

Incorrect response:	**Correct response:**
"Thank you."	"You seem to have some hesitation about recommending me. Do you mind if I ask about this?"

Dig deeper

Interviewer: "I was hoping to find someone with better computer skills."

Incorrect response:	**Correct response:**
"I use a computer in all of my classes."	"Do you mind if I ask exactly what kind of computer skills you are looking for?"

Remeasure

Interviewer: "I'm looking for someone who is Mac literate."

Incorrect response:	**Correct response:**
"I use a computer in all of my classes."	"So, the ideal candidate would have a general understanding of both the PC and the Mac?"

Target

Interviewer: "Yes, that's right."

Incorrect response:
"Great, I use both a PC and a Mac."

Correct response:
"Would the rest of my background fit your requirements if I were both PC and Mac literate?"

Pour

Interviewer: "Yes, I suppose so." (If no, repeat Steps 1 to 3.)

Incorrect response:
"Great, then will you be recommending me?"

Correct response:
"While all of my course work has been done on PCs, I have significant experience with the Mac. In fact, as chairman of the History Club, I do all of our work on a Mac."

Finish

Interviewer: "I see."

Incorrect response:
"Thank you for your time."

Correct response:
"Does that answer your concern?"

Close

Interviewer: "I guess it does."

Incorrect response:
"Thank you for your time."

Correct response:
"Great, thank you. Does this mean you will be recommending me for the next step?"

Interviewer: "I don't see why not."

You are assured of the next interview! DRM will always let you know where you stand and allow you to maintain control of the process.

Notes for *Closing the Sale:*

Notes for *Closing the Sale:*

> *"The person who makes a success of living is the one who sees his goal steadily and aims for it unswervingly. That is dedication."*
>
> — Cecil B. De Mille,
> legendary film director

Chapter 8

Setting Yourself Apart

The final step in the sales process is the follow-up. You may have heard the old saying, "the devil is in the details." This is true. Missing a key detail can undermine all of your other efforts. For instance, sending a follow-up note is crucial. People remember those who take the time to say "thank you." It's a thoughtful gesture that people respect. Sending a thank-you letter will set you apart from a large majority of your competitors who may not take the time to attend to this simple task.

However, sending a thank-you note alone will not necessarily give you a leg up on the competition. Others will also be thoughtful and do the same. So, to maintain an edge, you need to follow up *creatively*. Use your imagination to devise different methods, but be sure to remain professional at all times. Creative should not mean unprofessional.

One sure-fire way of getting an interviewer's attention when following up is to *exceed expectations*. Hundreds of books have been written on exceeding customer expectations. Businesses around the world swear that it is the only way to succeed.

What would the interviewer expect? What types of thank-you notes has he or she received in the past? What subjects are typically discussed in thank-you notes?

To exceed the interviewer's expectations, you need to *add something unexpected* to your thank-you note. Interviewers expect to be thanked for their time and to hear about your interest in the position. What an interviewer would not expect is to receive some useful information along with the note.

Exceeding Expectations

This exercise will help you focus on what an interviewer might expect for a follow-up. In addition to those listed below, what other expectations might an interviewer have?

What might the interviewer expect in a follow-up note?
- A "thank you" for his or her time.
- Some mention of your interest in the job.
- Some mention of topics discussed during the interview.
- _____
- _____
- _____
- _____
- _____

What might the interviewer expect in a follow-up phone call?
- A "thank you" for his or her time.
- A question about the status of the candidate search.
- _____
- _____
- _____
- _____
- _____

During your interview you probably covered several general topics related to the company's business. You might have discussed marketing strategies, new products, the competition, or one of many other topics. Armed with this information, you can now prove to the interviewer that you are a resource to their organization before you are actually an employee.

As a resource, your aim is to provide him or her with relevant and useful information. One way to do this is to attach to your thank-you note a newspaper or magazine article related to a topic you discussed during the interview. Be sure to staple the article to your thank-you note so that it cannot be mistakenly detached.

As previously discussed, gaining access to knowledge is very important in today's work world. If you have taken the time to find a relevant and useful article, you have proven yourself a knowledge resource. Any resource that provides knowledge cannot, and will not, be easily overlooked.

Once the interviewer has received your thank-you note and article, there are only four possible outcomes:

1. The interviewer finds it unprofessional. Both your thank-you note and article are thrown in the garbage.

2. He looks at the article, thinks it looks interesting, but doesn't have time to read it, so he sets it aside his desk. This is an extremely positive outcome. Your name and thank-you note will be on his desk and in his mind for quite some time.

3. He takes the time to read the article. If you have sent a relevant article, he will be impressed and appreciate that you provided him with useful information. Also, since he took the time to read the article, he spent much more time with your thank-you note than the 30 seconds it typically takes to read such a note.

4. He has already read the article. In this case, you sent an extremely powerful, subliminal message. The interviewer believes that you think about his business in the same way he does.

As you can see, three of these four possible outcomes will be positive — an excellent probability of success.

In order to make this work, you need to do a bit of homework. The first step is to locate a relevant article. A trip to your library or logging onto the Internet to conduct a topic search should provide you with exactly what you need. Seek out publications that target the interviewer's demographics. For example, if you are interviewing for a business position, a recent issue of *Business Week* could include a useful follow-up article. *The Wall Street Journal* is also a good source for timely articles on a variety of subjects.

Remember these key points for sending an article follow-up:

- Be sure to say thank-you in the letter.
- The article should be relevant to at least one of the following five topics:
    1. Something discussed during the interview.
    2. The company's business.
    3. Its competition.
    4. Its markets.
    5. Its business strategies.
- The article should be an information source to the interviewer, not to you.
- Send a good, clean copy.

Sample Thank-You Note

February 21, 20XX

Mr. Sean Joseph
Division Manager
XYZ Corporation
9635 Laurel Street
Mifflinwood, USA 11111

Dear Mr. Joseph:

Thank you for meeting with me on Monday. I am extremely excited about the opportunity to work for XYZ Corporation and am looking forward to continuing our discussions.

During the interview, we talked about the changes that are taking place in your industry. Based on our conversation, you may find the attached article of interest. This information has certainly given me more insight into the challenges and opportunities facing XYZ Corporation.

I will follow up with you on Monday, March 8. Please call me at (111) 555-2121 if you have any questions or need any additional information. Thank you again for your time.

Sincerely,

Jason Johnson

Jason Johnson

Enclosure

Is BIGGER Better?
Can a Mega-Corporation Maintain the Personal Touch?

Bob Perrin relates a story from one of his peers, a human resources person at a national restaurant chain, about creative follow-up.

"My friend was looking to hire a few fast-track college grads for regional positions, so he interviewed at several prestigious schools. His company also was looking to hire a few management candidates for local positions, and for these, he focused his recruiting efforts on the local public colleges.

"During an interview for one of the local positions, the candidate asked about expansion and product development. In his response, he mentioned the need to expand the dessert line with a more unique and upscale offering. The candidate asked a few more questions about product development and then they moved on to another subject.

"After the interview, my friend received a follow-up note from the candidate. Included was his grandmother's recipe for cheesecake. The candidate had also taken the time to shop the chain's competitors for upscale dessert offerings and found that no one was offering a quality cheesecake.

"The follow-up and research so impressed my friend that he called the candidate back in for additional interviews. In the end, this candidate displaced another graduate for one of the regional positions, even though he did not graduate from one of the more prestigious schools and wasn't initially being considered for the higher-level job."

This story illustrates two points: 1) the power of follow-up; and 2) the potential benefits of positioning yourself as a knowledge resource and problem-solver.

Following up is important, not only for interviews but also in the networking phase of your job search. After any contact, be it an interview or a networking meeting, you should follow up with a thank-you note. Attaching an interesting or relevant piece of information gives the note even more impact.

⌛ In addition to attaching a relevant article, what other ideas do you have for setting yourself apart through a follow-up letter?

- _____
- _____
- _____
- _____
- _____
- _____
- _____
- _____
- _____
- _____

At some point in your job search, you will also need or want to speak with a prospective employer over the telephone. There is a natural desire to refrain from doing this, the universal feeling being, "I don't want to be too aggressive," or, "I don't want to be a bother."

When a candidate does follow-up via telephone, and he doesn't get through or receive a call back, the tendency is to become discouraged. This only confirms his or her worst fears, causing an even greater hesitancy to follow up after future interviews.

Let's again come around to my side of the desk. I interviewed you on Monday, February 21. That was your third interview, and I told you that I would call you back in for a final interview. I said you would hear from me by "the end of the month."

By March 2, you have not heard anything. You summon up the courage to call and I do not call you back. Now, it's March 5. You are probably discouraged and have concluded that I am no longer interested. In fact, you decide against another contact, and you do not call back.

Now, let's look at the reality of my situation. I am still planning to make a hire, and have narrowed the field to three final candidates. You are one of these candidates. I have intended to call all three of you back to arrange a final interview. Each of you has called and left a message, which I have not returned.

Why haven't I called? Take a look at my calendar and see what my typical day looks like:

TIME	SUBJECT
7:00 a.m.	Catch up on reading
8:00 a.m.	Meeting with VP
9:30 a.m.	Finish report, due 5 p.m.
12:30 p.m.	Lunch
1:00 p.m.	Meeting with Advisory Council
3:00 p.m.	Client presentation
4:30 p.m.	Finalize and submit report
5:30 p.m.	Handle "B" priorities – review finalists

Do not become discouraged and do not stop calling. Simply change the time you call. As you can see by the calendar, there is no room for me to take unplanned calls. My schedule is just too tight. Everything I have planned is an "A" priority and must be addressed during the work day.

Early in the morning and after 5 p.m., I have set aside time to look at "B" priorities, such as when I first reviewed résumés. Before and after hours, I can relax a bit and think without having to deal directly with deadlines.

Now is the time to call. My work day is over, and I am unwinding. I have the time to talk. I didn't when you called at 8 a.m., as I was meeting with a vice president. If I don't want to take a phone call after 5 p.m., I will allow the call to go into my voice mail.

Therefore, you will either get me directly or indirectly through my voice mail. Leave me a succinct message. (See page 80-83.) Be sure to mention the time of day you called and when you will be available. I will then know that I can call you after hours, or during my "B" time. I will also see that we work the same type of schedule.

If I answer the phone, you can then speak to me directly. Since I am unwinding, I will have a few moments to talk. In fact, you will have done me a favor by calling, since I will not need to call you back to schedule a final interview.

You may have proven to be a resource. You may also have shown me that you are a time-conscientious professional. You have exceeded my expectations. If the other candidates stop following up, I might conclude that they are no longer interested. What will this do for your chances of landing the job?

A friend, Mike Lecak, recently decided to pursue a career change and discovered his dream job was available at a Fortune 50 company. He sent his résumé to a regional vice president, who was making the hiring decision. When he called a few days later to follow-up, my friend found that the vice president had not yet had the opportunity to review the résumé. But the vice president's assistant suggested that he fax a second résumé to another location, to which the vice president would be traveling later in the week. He followed this advice and then called that location to follow-up. Not only did he not get through, he didn't receive a return call, either.

Over the following eight weeks, my friend persistently called to follow-up. He left a voice mail message each time, but never received a call back. After each follow-up call, he would contact the assistant to make sure the job had not yet been filled.

Each voice mail message was scripted out in advance. Mike always left the time he had called, a succinct message, his return number and the time of day he could be reached. By his estimation, he called at least 15 times.

What Mike discovered after landing the job was that, in addition to his credentials, his follow-up set him apart. There had been other candidates for the position, but none of them had been as persistent.

The regional vice president had very good reasons for not calling back. His travel schedule regularly took him across different time zones, and he was in the middle of two high-profile projects. The times Mike indicated that he could be reached did not fit within the vice president's schedule. This being the case, he did not return the calls.

After completing the high profile projects, the vice president had the time to conduct interviews. Because of Mike's persistence, he was one of the few candidates still in hot pursuit of the job. His credentials, combined with his persistence, helped him to land his dream job.

Never assume the worst if you do not hear from an employer. Follow up in writing and over the phone. Be persistent, yet professional. Chances are, your competition will become discouraged. If you don't give up, you will be more likely to succeed.

Notes for *Setting Yourself Apart:*

> "What convinces is conviction. Believe in the argument you are advancing. If you don't, you are as good as dead. The other person will sense that something isn't there, and no chain of reasoning, no matter how logical or elegant or brilliant, will win your case for you."
>
> — Lyndon B. Johnson,
> 36th President of the United States

Chapter 9

Taking Control

There have been many articles written about the changing dynamics of an individual's career. The days of staying in one job forever, and then retiring, are long past. Every major corporation in America has come to realize this fact.

You are entering the job market at a very interesting point in history. The Industrial Revolution has given way to the Information Revolution which has, in turn, positioned you in the middle of a knowledge-based economy. Times are changing, the job market is changing, and the demands on employees are changing. All of this adds up to a wonderful opportunity for you.

Companies are beginning to teach employees — many of whom are in mid-career — to take control of their own destinies. Through this book you are learning this important concept *before* you begin your career. Remember, you are the only person in the world responsible for your career and for your ultimate professional success.

Once you have come to this realization, tapped into this opportunity, and implemented the ideas outlined in this book, you will be 20 years ahead of your mid-career counterparts. You will already know what needs to be done, and be prepared to take the necessary steps to reach your goals.

The current work environment will reward your efforts if you leverage the "3 R's":

1. Be aware of and **R**espect a person's time constraints.
2. Always **R**espond professionally and thoughtfully.
3. Become a knowledge **R**esource.

Respect time constraints. As we discussed in Chapter 1, time is a very valuable commodity in the professional world. There is never enough, and what there is must be maximized. The lack of time available to most professionals, however, shouldn't negatively impact your job search, if you can leverage it to your advantage. During your job search, demonstrate that you understand this market reality. Be early for your appointments and always provide appropriate, succinct information.

Remember these points of advice:

- An interviewer will only spend a few seconds reviewing your résumé, so make sure you write a specific job objective.
- Script and practice your telephone calls, including voice mail messages, in advance. Do not overlook this seemingly insignificant detail. Preparation equals professionalism.
- Record a succinct and professional outgoing message on your answering machine. Don't give the caller the impression that you are a time-waster.
- Most professionals' workdays are scheduled in advance with little time allotted for interruptions. Follow-up by telephone when "B" priorities are scheduled, before and/or after business hours.

Respond professionally. How you respond during each step of the hiring process is as critical as how you answer specific questions during an interview. Every interaction you have during your job search is a mini-interview. Treat these encounters as opportunities to maximize your chances for success.

- Prepare for all of your networking calls in advance. Be professional at all times, even if you are meeting informally. Wear your professional wardrobe. Most of all, be positive and do not use negative phraseology.
- Know your strengths and weaknesses. Be prepared to confidently talk through your funnels. Don't hide from or deny any failures. How you overcame and learned from your failures is the important point.
- Always ask questions during an interview. Failure to ask thoughtful questions will make you look as if you do not care about the opportunity. Learn how to use open-ended questions to advance a conversation.

- Be prepared to ask for the job or the next interview. Study the DRM method and be prepared to dig deeper, remeasure, target, pour and finish. If you don't, someone else might.
- Make sure your written correspondence represents you well. Carefully proofread your letters. Make sure that your letters not only say what you want, but also look professional. Do not send a letter with typos, erasures or smudge marks.
- Slowly read your correspondence out loud. Preferably, read it to another person. This will help you spot typos and identify improper punctuation.
- Always follow-up promptly. A quick response is positive, showing that you are interested. Nothing suggests disinterest like a delayed follow-up letter.

Be a knowledge resource. Next to time, the most precious commodity in today's professional environment is knowledge. A successful professional can never have enough information. This shortage of time forms the Decision-Makers Paradox: Decision-makers never have enough knowledge or time.

- Practice your CAR. Be able to smoothly display the results you can offer an organization. Knowing your CAR will underscore your problem-solving skills and abilities.
- Follow-up with everyone you meet during your job search. Through these follow-ups, seek to exceed expectations. Sending pertinent information or articles will highlight your ability to be an information source.

Take Control . . . Today

Begin preparing immediately for your job search. If you are still in school, examine the elective courses you are taking in terms of how they will help you find a job. Look at the clubs you join and how they will help you as you enter the work force? Do you do any charity work? How could being involved in a charitable project help you in the future? Have you looked into any internships? How will these internships set you apart? Do you become bored during spring break or holiday breaks? If so, can you find a job that gives you additional experience?

Having completed all the exercises in this book, you should be well prepared for every stage of your job search. As you get more experienced in the process, you should complete the exercises again. This will give you even more confidence. I firmly believe that the only difference between your reading this book, and my writing it, is my experience.

Finally, take time before your interviews to relax and visualize a positive outcome. How do you want to feel during the session? How will you feel afterwards? See yourself moving effortlessly through your funnels. Feel how confident you are using your CAR. See yourself asking and receiving a positive response to your closing questions.

By visualizing your success, you are sending your brain a very powerful message. Visualization creates a positive mental picture deep in your subconscious. This picture acts as your road map through the interview. Your conscious mind will instinctively follow this road map. If you do not give your conscious self a guide, you will be less likely to be successful. Just as a professional golfer sees and feels the next shot, try to see and feel a positive outcome. It really works!

If I can ever be of any help, let me know. You can contact me through the Solutions 21 Web site (www.solutions-21.com). E-mail me your résumé. (I might have a contact who would be interested in seeing it.) Also, let me know about your success. Did you find a job? How did this book help? How can I improve upon it to help future graduates? I would love to get your feedback.

I know some of the items contained in this book are going to be difficult to implement, but I also know that you have the courage to do it. If you did not have the courage, you would not have made it this far.

A long time ago, someone shared with me a very inspirational quotation. I want to close this book by passing it along. I hope it will provide you with the same ongoing inspiration it has provided me.

Man In The Arena

It is not the critic who counts; not the man who points out how the strong man stumbles, or where the doer of deeds could have done them better. The credit belongs to the man in the arena, whose face is marred by dust and sweat and blood; who strives valiantly...who knows the great enthusiasms, the great devotions; who spends himself in a worthy cause; who at the best knows in the end the triumph of high achievement, and who at the worst, if he fails, at least fails while daring greatly, so that his place shall never be with those cold and timid souls who have never known neither victory nor defeat.

— Theodore Roosevelt,
26th President of the United States,
author, conservationist

Recommended Reading

Arredondo, Lani. *How to Present Like a Pro!: Getting People to See Things Your Way.* McGraw-Hill, Inc. New York, N.Y. (1991).

Cohen, Steve and de Oliveira, Paulo. *Getting to the Right Job.* Workman Publishing, Inc. New York, N.Y. (1987).

Fein, Richard. *First Job: A New Grad's Guide to Launching Your Business Career.* John Wiley & Sons, Inc. New York, N.Y. (1992).

Kalish, Karen. *How to Give a Terrific Presentation.* AMACOM. New York, N.Y. (1997).

LaFevre, John L. *How to Really Get Hired: The Inside Story from a College Recruiter.* 3rd edition. Prentice Hall.
New York, N.Y. (1992).

Lewis, David. *The Secret Language of Success: Using Body Language to Get What You Want.* Carroll & Graff Publishers. New York, N.Y. (1990).

Molloy, John T. *New Dress For Success.* Warner Books, Inc. New York, N.Y. (1988).

Molloy, John T. *New Woman's Dress For Success.* Warner Books, Inc., New York, N.Y. (1996).

Index

"3 R's", 165
Activities and organizations, 18, 22, 23, 30, 31, 32, 33, 35, 39, 40, 41, 42, 52-55, 64, 127
Adversity/failure, overcoming, 36-37, 43
Advertising campaign, 101
Advice, asking for, 94, 96
Annual reports, 73
Answering machine, See telephone
Baby Boomers, 2-4
Bacon, Francis, 88
"B" priorities, 12, 161, 166
Breathing, 121, 122
Burnett, Leo, 10
Business Week, 156
CAR (Component-Advantage-Result), 131-132, 134-137, 167, 168
Career goals, 30, 31, 32, 35, 60-63
Closing the sale, 113, 141-149
Communication skills, 79-80, 122-128, 133
    interpersonal communication, 122-128
    non-verbal communication, 114-115
    tone of voice, 115, 121
Competitors, 72, 74, 75, 76, 159
Components of a product, 131-132, 134-137
Computerworld Magazine, 122
Conceptual thinking, 4-5

Confidence, 36-37, 64, 124, 132, 142, 168
Co-operative education assignment, 18
Courage, 6-8, 32, 73, 126, 128, 141-142, 144, 160, 168
Cover letters, 11, 101-104, 107-109
Creative research, 71-79
Current employees, contacting, 79
De Mille, Cecil B., 152
Decision-makers
    Decision-Maker's Paradox, V, 167
    Today's/Twenty-First Century IV, V, 1-5
    Yesterday's, 3-4, 5
Determining a match, 114, 124
Direct mail campaign, 104
DRM (Dream Retirement Method), 144-149, 167
Educational background, 13, 20-23, 30-31, 34, 39, 48-51, 102, 123
E-mail, 3, 4, 13-14, 22-23, 89, 90
E-Span, 90
Evolution of business, IV, 1-5, 11
Exceeding expectations, 153-159
Face-to-face meeting, 79, 80, 85, 110
Failed interviews, 123
Failure, See adversity
Fear, overcoming, 6-7, 36, 141, 144, 160

Feedback, 66, 105, 117, 122, 168
Follow-up letter/note, *See* letters
Fortune 500, VI, 14
Funnels, 30-67, 79, 124, 131, 166, 168
Golf tournament analogy, 126, 128
Grade-point average (GPA), 34, 39, 48, 93
Graduating in four years vs. five years, 36
Great Depression, 3
Handshake, 115, 120-121, 122
Help-wanted ads, *See* newspapers
Hidden job market, 92
HR Magazine, 114
Human resources professionals, 122
IBM, 124-126, 128
Industrial Revolution, 165
Information Revolution, 165
Institute of Management, 11
Internet, 76
   Web sites, 14, 72
Internships, 18, 41, 60, 102, 108, 167
Interviews, 29, 30-67, 71-72, 73, 79, 80, 81, 85, 90, 107-108, 110, 113-137, 142-149, 156-157, 166-167
Interviewers, 29, 30, 31, 32, 33, 34, 36, 37, 43, 64, 65, 72, 73, 75, 79, 113-114, 116, 121, 123, 124, 125, 126, 127, 128, 129, 130, 134, 142, 143, 144, 145, 146, 147, 148-149, 153, 154, 155, 156, 166

Job Choices, 90
Job objective, 12, 13, 14, 15, 19, 20-23, 166
Job search tactics, 3-4
Jobnet, 90
JobTrak, 90
Jobwire, 90
Johnson, Lyndon B., 164
KBS (Knowledge-Based Sales), IV, V
Knight, Bobby, 70
Knowledge resource, becoming a, 72, 73, 155, 159, 165, 167
Leadership
   roles, 18, 33
   skills, 17, 52, 133
Lecak, Mike, 161
Letters
   introduction, of, 85
   writing, 79
   follow-up letter/note, 153-159, 167
Listening skills, 123, 124, 133
Mackay, Harvey, 1, 95
Mail five, phone five strategy, 104
Marketing campaign, 2, 5
Microsoft, 130
Monster Board, 90
Musashi, Miyamoto, 140
Nervousness, overcoming, 29, 65, 66
Network truths, 101, 104, 110
Networking, 92-110

Newspapers, 89, 90
Non-verbal communication, 114-115
Objections, overcoming, 141, 144-149
One Step Away List, 96-100
On-line career fairs, 90
Open-mindedness, 101, 106
Opportunities for recent college graduates, 1
Pacino, Al, 95
Paraphrasing answers, 66, 67
Perrin, Robert, 71-72, 158
Persistence, 162
Personal background information, 30
Peters, Tom, VI
Placement office, 11, 73, 85, 89, 107, 129
Potential employers, identifying, 89-100
Practice, 25, 64-67, 71, 80-83, 84, 132, 134, 166, 167
Preparing for an interview, 29
Pritchard, David, 130
Problem solving, 48, 71, 114, 130-132, 133, 147, 167
Professional dress, 116-119
Professionalism, 110, 142, 166
Prospecting, 89-110
Qualifications, 90, 107, 108, 109, 113, 143, 144, 145
Quarterly reports, 73
Questions, 30-31, 33, 36, 37, 65, 74-75, 105, 110, 122-123, 124, 125, 127, 128, 129, 130, 142, 143, 145, 166, 168
    Closed-ended, 126-127
    Multi-part, 123-124
    Open-ended, 126-127, 166
Rather, Dan, 112
References, 20-23, 96-110, 143
Rejection letters, 13, 15, 125, 142, 143
Résumés, 11-12, 13, 14, 15, 16, 20-23, 24, 25, 33, 64, 73, 89, 90, 93, 96, 104, 105, 107, 110, 113, 127, 131, 134, 142, 161, 166, 168
Roosevelt, Theodore, 169
Sales professionals, IV, V, 130, 131, 141
Self-inventory, 16-17, 19, 34
Skills employers are seeking, 133, 134
Solutions 21, IV, 95, 114
Statistics, 71, 72
Stock, purchasing, 74
Strengths and weaknesses, 7-8, 16, 34, 79, 128, 166
Tape recorder, using, 65, 67, 84
Target market, 3, 14, 71
Targeting a response, 145-146, 149
Teamwork, 52, 133
Telephone
    answering machines, 25
    follow-up phone calls, 154, 162
    script, 80-83
    skills, 79-81

controlling your airwaves, 24-25
voice mail 81, 84, 161, 166
Thank-you note, *See* letters, follow-up letter/note
Time constraints, respecting, 13, 24, 165-166
Tone of voice, *See* communication
Transitional phrases, 132
Tunie, Tamara, 95
Video camera, using, 66
Voice mail, *See* telephone
Wall Street Journal, 156
Web sites, *See* Internet
What employers look for, 16, 18, 34
What you know vs. who you know, 93
Why employers will pay more, 16, 18, 34
Wiley, Raymond, 24
Work experience, 13, 16, 18, 20-23, 30, 31, 32, 33, 35, 41, 56-59, 66
Xerox, III

About the Author

John W. "Buddy" Hobart is founder and president of Solutions 21, a Pittsburgh-based company providing strategic business planning services, customized training programs and a full line of training products for businesses. He founded the company on the belief that "people will provide the solutions in the twenty-first century." Today, Solutions 21 works with companies ranging in size from Inc. 500 to Fortune 500 and also serves a number of international clients.

Throughout his career, Mr. Hobart has been internationally recognized for the development of several innovative marketing programs. He is a co-author of the book *Celebrate Selling*, an informative sales handbook. In addition, he has served as a consultant to many Fortune 500 companies, including Lanier Worldwide, KPMG Peat Marwick, Coopers & Lybrand, USX, Pfizer and Eckerd Health Services.

As a noted expert and lecturer on job search techniques and career management, Mr. Hobart regularly addresses both college students and established professionals on the changing landscape of the working world.

A graduate of Carnegie Mellon University, he lives in Oakdale, Pa.

Once you've landed your first job, learn to do it better with:

MEETINGS: DO'S, DON'TS AND DONUTS
The Complete Handbook for Successful Meetings
by Sharon M. Lippincott

Learn everything you need to know about conducting effective meetings that get results. From agendas to follow-up, this handy reference covers it all.

Who should (and shouldn't) be invited to meetings for maximum productivity.
What to do when negative attitudes influence the meeting.
Where to hold a meeting for the results you want.
When and **How** to exert leadership from the sidelines to keep things on track.

Retail Price: $16.95 U.S.	**Special Offer:**	2 books for $30.50 U.S. *(Save 10%)*

Corporate Sales: Please call for information on special corporate editions.
Phone: (412) 323-9320.

Shipping:
Book Rate: Add $2.50 for shipping for first book and $1 for each additional book. (Surface shipping may take three to four weeks.)

Priority Shipping: $5 for up to two books (please call for priority shipping information on more than two books)

Terms: Payment with order.

Please send me _____ copy/ copies of *Meetings: Do's, Don'ts and Donuts.*

Name:_____
Address:_____
City:_____State:_____Zip:_____

Sales Tax: Please add 7% sales tax for books shipped to Pennsylvania address.

Amount Enclosed: _____

Send check or money order to: **Lighthouse Point Press**
700 River Ave.
Pittsburgh, PA 15212